MW01173220

The
RED
Quarters

Gina Panzino

The Red Quarters

ISBN: 979-8-89316-691-0 - Paperback
ISBN: 979-8-89316-692-7 - Hardcover
ISBN: 979-8-89316-690-3 - eBook

In honor and loving memory
of my Daddy

Forever your
Poohbear

CONTENTS

Introduction

A picture of Daddy in front of me, on my desk. A small wooden box filled with my treasures. Gifts from heaven. Proof that Daddy is still with me.

I sit here remembering the good times. Visions of him healthy playing over and over in my mind. Flashes of his laughter echoing in my head just as they used to vibrate throughout our entire home. Countless wonderful memories and valuable life lessons which inevitably shaped me into the person I am today. I'm overwhelmed with gratitude that he was mine, and I was his. I feel blessed for my first twenty-seven years as his daughter.

I was born in the winter of 1972. My sister, Dawn, was five years old. I was told when my father walked in to see me for the first time, I was in my mother's arms with Dawny standing beside the hospital bed. Daddy smiled with pride looking at the three of us.

And from that moment on the three of us were *his girls.*

My father was a banker. Every Monday through Saturday he would walk into his little office with a big smile for everyone. Dressed in a suit and tie complete with his gold chain to honor the blessed mother, bracelets and rings, his leather suitcase in hand. He was approachable, kind, friendly, respected and loved by his employees and his customers.

The job itself was stressful with unexpected mergers over the years, but he loved the opportunity to help hard-working, good people get the loans they needed to make their lives better for their own families. He worked hard for his family in order to provide whatever he could for *his girls.*

My beautiful mother adored him and was a traditional, loving wife. When we were young, she worked part-time so she could pick us up from school, make dinners and iron Daddy's work shirts.

Theirs was a love most envied. They cherished one another and truly were soulmates. Over the years, our family had their ups and downs like everyone's does. Moving into new homes, parents changing jobs and my sister and I making friends. The typical Italian, Catholic family. Girls in Catholic school, hard working parents, in-laws next door, a miniature collie and two goldfish. We were happy.

What could possibly go wrong?

My eyes sting, and there's a lump in my throat. I try to fight back the tears with little success as they stream down my face.

Oh, daddy. How I still wish you were here.

I battle the ongoing obstacles of day-to-day life. The bills, parenting alone, raising a child with special needs, working as a teacher full-time and running a household. A full-time teacher, single mom of two amazing kids and a writer at heart. Summer break affords me the time to reflect on, grow and share my story. I strive to make the best out of every day. I aim to care for, love and protect my family and friends, honoring Daddy's example.

I wonder how many times I can stand back up after getting knocked down in my lifetime. How many more setbacks before success? How many more heartbreaks must I endure?

God has blessed me with loving and supportive family and friends.

My beautiful mother is thoughtful, kind and generous.

I sit here wondering what our lives would be like if he were still here with us today. I imagine how incredibly different my life would be.

He has four amazing grandchildren that never had the pleasure of feeling his love. They never felt his arms wrap them up in his love. They never experienced his voice echo through the stadium or across the court as he cheered for his kids.

The hairs on my arms stand tall at the altered reality I often imagine.

My Daddy taught me so much during my twenty seven years while he was on this Earth.

One of the many things I loved about him was his ability to teach and lead by example. I rarely remember times he told me what to do or how to behave. He had a loving, gentle way of demonstrating the person I should become. He rarely yelled. Come to think of it, he didn't yell at us. He had a look. That look said it all.

It was an adorable, slightly humorous look with a wide side-eye stare and twisted mouth as if to say, "Seriously, G? Are you kidding me?" And somehow, that look was always enough to get his point across.

I, of course, would reply to his look with whatever the excuse of the day was for my misbehavior. To which he'd retort with a calm explanation of why it was a bad choice. I'd end up apologizing and hugging him.

I don't know how many of you experienced such a calm, loving father with a strong influence that never angered you, but if you are blessed like I was with a Daddy like mine, I believe we are the minority.

Knowing his past of a tumultuous upbringing, it has always impressed me how he was always strong yet gentle, influential but not pushy, strict yet never mean. To say I miss him even after twenty-five years is a gross understatement.

There are days, even after all this time, my heart truly aches for him. I long for our life talks about how to handle a difficult situation. His booming laughter and contagious smile are intensely missed.

The patience and kindness he regularly displayed and the love he always showed my sister, my mom and I are what we still miss daily.

Over the years, we've shared our stories of the red quarters with friends, family and coworkers. Each time they have been blessed and inspired to believe. The red quarters give others hope and, in my mind, provide proof that our past loved ones are with us in our time of need. That they see us struggle and share in our celebrations and comfort us during difficult times, even after they have passed on.

There have been many movies, books and interviews about life after death. Some are skeptical or some vehemently disagree that such a wonder is possible. While others want to believe and ask many questions secretly hoping that just one response will fill their hearts with knowing it is possible.

My goal for this book is to share our personal, true stories, knowing that many of you will be blessed with God's gift of truly believing.

Furthermore, it is my hope that this book provides comfort to those of you who are suffering with immense grief.

One red quarter may be a coincidence. Several in various towns, given to many people over the course of a quarter century, is proof to me.

I can still see his handsome face with that sideways smirk without even closing my eyes.

Twenty-five years have gone by.

I remember it like it was yesterday.

Losing my Daddy changed the trajectory of my life forever.

After all these years, I close my eyes and can still remember where it all went so horribly wrong.

CHAPTER 1

My World Stopped

As I sat on a musty couch, surrounded by hundreds of people, I never felt more alone.

Scores of blurred faces passed by, hugging my mother and sister and bending over me to squeeze my hand with condolence. Fuzzy silhouettes of men and women in black lined the walls and wrapped down the hall as far as the eye could see.

I couldn't see clearly or focus, although I tried. My eyes stung as I tried to fight back tears, to no avail. As they streamed down my face, I wiped my face with my hands and exhaled strongly, not realizing until then I had been holding my breath. I didn't make eye contact with many people and all the surrounding conversations became a dull hum. I couldn't see anything or anyone.

Nothing except the old-looking, frail man who lay in front of me in a casket. He was so unrecognizable I could allow myself to think it was someone else. This surely was not the vibrant man I had idolized for the past twenty-seven years.

Feeling exhausted and confused, I tried to make sense of what was happening.

That wasn't him.

Why are we here?

There has to be a mistake.

This is not happening.

These people should not be here.

Cars filled with family and friends poured into the driveway of the funeral home. Later I was told, local police had to direct the cars as the vehicles ceaselessly spilled into the road, blocking the daily traffic.

It was clear to everyone, by the vast crowds, that all who knew him truly admired and loved him. It was an impressive display and a magnificent tribute.

I occasionally caught the tear-filled eyes of a dear friend, an aunt or cousin. They'd look in my direction with great sorrow and although I felt disoriented, I somehow appreciated the love and support. My mind again began searching for an explanation.

What am I doing here?

What is happening?

What these people are saying cannot be true.

It's not him!

God wouldn't do this to me.

Innumerable waves of people continued to walk past. They'd kneel in front of him, to pay their respects, only to rise crying and immediately grab my mother and hug my sister.

I sat in the front on a large leather couch, too distraught to stand alongside my mother, my sister, our husbands and my maternal grandparents.

Somewhere in my gut I knew it was him, but my mind was in such a fog and my heart just wouldn't accept it. Growing more and more angry and still feeling disoriented, I closed my eyes and prayed.

Dear God, what is happening?

I don't understand what all these people are doing here.

That's not him.

That can not be him!

It's not my Daddy.

It's not my Daddy!

What have You done!?!

I begged You not to do this. I have pleaded with You countless times over the past two years and begged you not to allow this to happen.

What have You done!?

You can't have him!

He's mine!

Memories then flashed through my mind to a time when I was about five years old. Sitting on daddy's knee, face to face with that loving smile of his ear to ear. He was clearly having an even greater time of it than I, although I couldn't imagine how that was possible. After all, my daddy hung the moon. As he tapped his foot on the ground, bouncing me up and down, securely holding both of my hands, he sang to me,

Pony girl, pony girl, won't you be my pony girl?

Marry me. Carry me, far across the sea.

Giddy up… giddy up… giddy up… giddy up! WhoOOaaa my pony girl!

And by the last line, the bouncing was more pronounced, and he leaned me back, as I arched backwards and then swiftly pulled me into his chest for a great big, warm hug.

The dedicated father who had always enveloped me with his love, who repeatedly sat, front and center, at every dance recital and in football stadiums watching his little girl cheer, with his infectious smile and beaming with pride… now lay lifeless, in front of me, in a casket.

That's not him.

That can't be him.

That's NOT my daddy!

The torturing hours went by as if time could convince me of this new, horrible reality. My aching neck grew tighter with every sorrowful handshake or hug, bringing me out of my fog long enough to chat with a few mourners. I dreaded having to make conversation and after a short time of attempting to speak to them; I sunk back into the couch, where I was safe in my warped reality.

I never felt so alone.

Countless people surrounded my mother, who appeared as if trapped in her own torture chamber of grief. His wife. His soulmate. I had never seen her look so haggard. My heart literally felt as if it broke for her. Still not quite allowing my thoughts to acknowledge why. Many others enveloped my sister, Dawn, with sorrowful hugs. She was seven months pregnant with his first grandchild.

The focus was on them. I understood, of course. My poor mother was beyond devastated and completely inconsolable. I was extremely worried about my sister and how this trauma would affect my unborn niece.

My grandparents worried me, as well. Crying and shaking periodically. Nonni didn't leave her daughter's side, from what I could tell. And every time I looked over at Poppop, he was fighting back tears or had his head in his hands. They were in their seventies and not in the best of health. And although they were Mommy's parents, Daddy was truly like a son to them. They had always lived right down the street from us and by the time I was seven; they lived with us in their own apartment, built just for them, connected to our home till this day. My father respected and loved them like they were his own parents.

As I held onto my family, I cried for their hurt. I sobbed with them because I could feel their immense pain.

I wanted to be with my Daddy wherever *he* was. Aching thoughts of wanting him here with all of us rushed through my mind over and over and over again. We did everything together. He was joy, laughter and love and the epitome of a terrific husband and an amazing father.

I kept thinking…

I want to be with him. I want him here with me now. I didn't want to be here with these confused, pitiful people. I thought I must be dreaming. An awful, terrifying nightmare… but why wasn't I waking up?

The thought that my amazing father, elated to be a grand pop, would never get to hold his first grandchild, a precious baby girl, was too cruel of a thought to accept.

Everyone feared this day for two years, except me.

I didn't cry all the time like everyone else. I didn't listen to anyone who talked about how he was deteriorating. I didn't expect this. I just never believed it would happen.

It doesn't matter how old you are when you lose a parent. The loss is devastating. I was twenty-seven. It was too soon.

Daddy was only fifty-six years old.

I never thought that God would do that to me. He knew how much I loved, admired and adored him. He knew how his care and thoughtfulness guided my decisions in life. God knew how Daddy always supported my choices. He knew the joy, the laughter, and the unconditional love my father provided me. I was 'the little one', his spitting image, his pony girl bouncing on his knee, his ballerina.

I was his Pooh bear.

I had begged, pleaded and bargained with God to use Daddy to glorify Him, to prove that miracles happen through prayer. I believed He would hear me, in the depths of my soul. I never thought, for a minute of those torturous two years, that He would take my Daddy away from me.

I eventually stood up from the leather couch to stretch my legs and work that kink out of my strained neck. It had been hours, although I had no idea what day it was or if it was daytime or evening. I felt something. As if an unexplained force pulled me and I began taking a few steps forward. My eyes fixed on that poor, frail man that lay in front of me.

By the time I reached the casket, I felt my sister's hand on my arm. I didn't look at her but could tell she was sobbing. My eyes fixed on his face.

Your sunken, pale face looks so old.

You used to be tan and handsome.

There's no smile either.

Wake up.

I exhaled aloud, again not realizing I'd been holding my breath.

I placed my hand on his.

It was so cold.

Tears streamed down my face.

Then, suddenly, it was as if a bolt of lightning struck me, in the center of my chest.

Then, I felt my heart break.

Daddy?

CHAPTER 2

The Early Years

Music and laughter permeated throughout the den of our modest ranch home. Family and friends chattered away with drinks in hand. Everyone was enjoying the holiday together. Traditional red and green decorations draped every surface with great care in each room. What, to a five-year-old, seemed like a massive Christmas tree stood proudly in the corner with sparkling lights and matching ornaments–it was a true beauty to behold.

Though I remember little of my early youth, this is a scene I'll always hold dear. Christmas carols on large albums were spinning on the record player. I happily twirled and danced around our many guests. I was quite the performer, even at five.

It was Christmas 1977.

The Christmas party was definitely one of those times Daddy grinned from ear to ear. In fact, any time friends and family surrounded him, he beamed with joy. Nothing pleased him more than to be surrounded by those he held dear.

My parents would have people over for the smallest occasions. But hands down, his absolute favorite time of year was Christmas.

Christmas was the *main event.* It was the best time of the year; my parents pulled out all the stops. For us, it literally began the day after Thanksgiving.

Beautiful, classy, festive and religious decorations removed carefully from their boxes with attentiveness. Frank Sinatra, Dean Martin and Tony Bennett beguiled us as we embellished every room together, decorating as a family.

The music, delicious home-cooked Italian meals, and being surrounded by his family and beloved friends were the special moments that made Daddy thrive.

The roar of his laughter echoed from one room into the other. He was at his best and happiest surrounded by his loved ones and, of course, with all of *his girls* by his side.

At this particular Christmas party, I don't recall if it was a Sunday or not, but everyone dressed up in their church clothes. I remember Dawn and I were showing off our matching red, green, and tan plaid rompers that our Nonni made for us by hand. I loved matching my big sister! I'm pretty sure, being five years older, she hated it, but she would have never told me that.

My beautiful mother, dressed in all red with matching lipstick, entered the room with her sweet smile. She had smooth, jet black hair that she'd flatten with a clothes iron to straighten. It curled under softly at the ends, very Jackie-O-like. Not aware of her beauty, every hair in place, she looked over at Daddy, and he beamed with pride. Gold dangled from her ears and draped her slender neck besides sentimental bracelets and rings all given to her by my father over eleven years of anniversaries and birthdays. I remember thinking she resembled Marlo Thomas from *That Girl* but, in my eyes, even more beautiful. In my eyes, she looked perfect.

Dawny and I sported our frizzy curls that Mommy had tried to smooth straight for us but, to no avail, feathered back off to the sides.

It was time for pictures. Everyone took turns in front of the fireplace wall. It was red and brown brick from floor to ceiling with a ledge perfect for the little ones, like me, to stand on. It wasn't often we posed for pictures at home. That was usually a once a year thing at the local Sears or school picture day at Sacred Heart. But someone, I don't remember who, had a camera at our Christmas party, and I was so excited.

The big cube on top of the camera flashed as the button clicked. Then they winded the dial in the back so it was ready to go for the next shot.

The small den, packed with friends and family snacking on hors d'oeuvres and sipping on festive drinks, grew louder with each hour that passed. As I was jumping up and down with excitement and dancing to the record player, Dean Martin sang, "A Marshmallow World". Daddy thought it would be cute if 'the little one' — that was me — would stand inside the giant, red stocking.

In all the commotion, apparently, I hit Uncle Ronnie in the face and knocked his drink out of his hand as he held the stocking for me to climb inside. It clearly was an accident. Everyone knew I didn't mean to, especially my Daddy.

He was very calm and whispered to me, "Pooh bear, say you're sorry."

I felt embarrassed at first, and then nervous, about how to apologize. Noticing my anxiety, Daddy put his arms around me.

"I know it was an accident. Everyone knows you didn't do it on purpose," he whispered sweetly, "But it's good manners to say you're sorry when you bump into someone. You're not in trouble."

I immediately felt relieved and quickly apologized for the accident. Uncle Ron had already moved on and seemed like it was no big deal at all.

But I learned, in that moment, about manners and saying you're *sorry* or *excuse me* in order to be considerate to others. It's a tough lesson when you're only five years old, but Daddy made it easier. He always made everything okay.

After I said I was sorry to Uncle Ronnie, Daddy smiled that great big smile of his, and with a twinkle in his eye, said, "That's my Pooh bear. Great job. Daddy loves you," which, of course, erased any remnant of embarrassment.

Always calm and kind. Always showing care and concern for my feelings. Always with love.

There were many other nights my parents had their friends over for parties for what seemed like no other reason than to play music and dance in the living room. My generation of friends, Dawn, Billy, Shelly, Lisa and Lori, have fond memories of what we now refer to as 'The Dance Parties at the Panzino's.'

One night in particular, Daddy picked up Lori to dance with her. She was only about four years old at the time. As they danced with her legs swinging in the air to "Sweet Gypsy Rose" and "Rock the Boat", they both sang and laughed together. Something that clearly made a positive impression on her given the fact she retells the story many decades later.

Lori's sister, Lisa, remembers how Daddy – 'Sammy' as she called him – taught her to play chess at one of those parties.

He was Salvatore, or Sal, to work associates and acquaintances, but close friends always called him Sammy.

I felt so proud watching how he loved my friends. It's because of my Daddy, Lisa knows how to play chess and Lori has wonderful, fun memories of good times with him. What an honor. He gave so much love and kindness to everyone.

Feelings of safety surrounded by extended family, love and laughter consumed my early years. I will forever feel blessed and grateful for my childhood. But as most teens do, I started to revolt against the rules and tried to carve my own path at any expense. My friends and activities were my priority. Sometimes, even if the answer was no, I'd find a way to get what I wanted. If it weren't for my parents checking up on me and my big sis keeping me out of trouble, I'm not sure where I'd be now.

To this day, Dawny tells stories of how I got away with everything. She paved the way for me where my parents were concerned, and, according to her, I was allowed to do much more than she ever was. Which understandably annoyed the crap out of her. I'd prefer to say I was high-spirited. Admittingly having much more freedom than my older sister, I still felt as though I was always in their protective bubble.

In the summers, we spent all of our free time at the Capri Swim Club. The neighborhood pool was at the end of our road, and the swim coach lived across the street. It was a tight-knit community, and all our neighbors became good friends and still are to this day.

One day at Capri, I was getting ready to start lessons. The coach was already in the pool, and I remember feeling a little nervous.

Daddy gave me a pep talk and said, “No sweat, Pooh.”

And with that, he picked me up and threw me into the pool. I wasn’t even scared. I trusted him implicitly.

Coach was right there cheering me on, and I swam. Not with any amount of grace or skill, but I kept my head above water and made my way to the other side.

When I looked back, Daddy had a huge smile and was yelling, “Atta girl, Pooh! I knew you could do it!”

The next thing I knew, I was on the swim team, and my parents told everyone I swam like a fish.

I cannot count how many times I’ve thought about my father always believing in me. I’ve accomplished so much in my life thinking…

If Daddy thought I could do anything, I guess I can.

My confidence soared after that summer. And with the support of my parents, I was so excited to begin dance classes. After all, Dawny was at the same dance studio. I admired my big sis so much and tried desperately to emulate her.

My parents enrolled me in dance classes with Maxine Chapman at her local studio. She was an old

Vineland High School classmate of Daddy's. He would have never trusted his little girl to just anyone, God-forbid a stranger. No, no. It had to be an old friend. So that's where his girls went. I loved dancing from day one. I felt so happy on stage.

Year after year, my parents were front and center at every recital clapping and smiling proudly. He would always make sure they went early enough to get the best seats with the best view, and he always had his camera ready.

Daddy would often stand and yell out to me, "That's my girl! Yeah, Pooh!"

I felt proud of myself. That was one of my earliest experiences feeling a sense of accomplishment and pride in a job well done. Another wonderful example of how his love, encouragement and support helped me achieve my goals and gain confidence.

It didn't end there.

The bragging went on for weeks after a performance. He made sure to get the film developed as soon as possible. He would share the pictures at Sunday family dinners, and everyone would mark on the back of pictures they wanted copies of. Daddy would happily return to the store and buy more copies of *his girls* to give out to the rest of the family.

Daddy was always so proud of '*his girls*'. All three of us. Mommy, my big sister and me. We were *his girls*. I cannot tell you how many times I heard him utter the phrase *my girls*.

Can't make it tonight. I'm having dinner with my girls.

Did you see how beautiful my girls *looked at the party?*

My girls *are the best.*

My girls *are such great dancers.*

I'm planning a vacation for my girls.

Many summers we enjoyed a week in Sea Isle City, NJ.

Digging in the sand and building sand castles from my bright pink molded bucket as Mommy and Daddy basked in the sun. Giant sunglasses and a floppy black hat covered most of Mommy's face while Daddy sprawled out without any concern of burning. When he needed to cool off, Daddy would escort me and Dawny into the ocean. We were always carefully positioned near a lifeguard but still never allowed to enter the ocean without Daddy protectively by our side. Once I was waist deep, Daddy would take me by the hand so I could go out even further with him. The waves crashed over my head as they tossed my skinny body around, and just as I tried to resurface, I felt Daddy grab my arm and pull me above water, safe in his arms. We'd battle the waves for what seemed like hours..

Every night of the vacation provided us with fun-filled games in the arcade–throwing softballs to knock down the bottles, scores of tickets streaming out of the skeeball machine, stuffed animal prizes followed by relaxing walks on the promenade. But the carousel was one of our absolute favorite activities.

Spinning around, I tried to find my mother's face every go around. She was always standing in the crowd juggling all of our jackets and snacks with her parents, Nonni and Poppop, smiling beside her. We always went on vacations–the six of us all together.

Music blared along with yelling and laughter of the crowds of happy moms, dads and children with cotton candy or ice cream in hand as far as the eye could see. My horse went up and down, opposite of Daddy's. He always rode the horse on the outside, reaching his arm off the side as the carousel turned towards the prize. A giant, metal arm outreached towards the horses with coveted metal rings waiting to be grabbed.

Laughing the whole time and filled with anticipation, I excitedly waited for my hero to capture the magical ring and hand it to me with his infectious smile of pride and joy. Daddy would ride that carousel as long as it took to be sure to get a ring for each of *his girls*.

Whenever someone asked about his family, he always responded by saying *my girls* did this and *my girls* did that and *my girls*.... People who knew him well knew exactly who he was referring to. And every time he said it, a delighted expression would cover his tan, chiseled Italian face... *bella faccia*.

Mommy, Dawn and I were his entire world. We all felt his immense love as much as he felt it for each of us. He made us feel as if we were up on a pedestal. We felt seen, heard and treasured.

He continued to work hard, and his efforts paid off. In what seemed like no time at all, he received a promotion to branch manager. And with that, we were off to 'bigger and better' places as a family.

Dawn was less than thrilled to share a bedroom with her energetic, needy little sister. Even though it was the entire width of the back of the house, my parents knew it would be an issue. Understanding that a teenage girl needed her space, they had a wall put up to divide the space into two large, separate rooms. I clearly remember, after the construction worker's installed the studs. I thought it was great to lay in bed, at night, and still be able to see and talk to my sister.

I can see you, Dawny!

Yes, G. I see you too. Now go to sleep.

The Spanish-style, large two-story home was orange stucco complete with archways around the front porch and the large carport in the back of the house. A beautiful, black wrought-iron balcony graced the front of the home above the front door. My parents had access to the private deck from their master bedroom.

Inside, as you opened the front door, a wide sweeping staircase curved upward. The black, wrought-iron railing with an intricate design swirled upward towards the second floor and overlooked the foyer. A massive black, wrought-iron gate divided the majestic staircase from the hallway to the bedrooms. I was only six years old, but awe-struck just the same, as we moved into this beautiful, much bigger home.

Few would doubt its beauty, but truth be told, my parents were a little (okay a lot) overprotective. They had learned, in my six short years, that I was a sleepwalker. They were so concerned — having now moved from a small rancher to such a large two-story home — that daddy had the iron gate installed. He did whatever he could to protect *his girls.* So I wouldn't fall down the stairs in a midnight slumber, the gate always got locked when everyone turned in for the night.

They were very perceptive.

Low and behold, one evening, in the middle of the night, as I stumbled around in my sleep, I made my way to the stairs. Of course, I didn't know how to open the child-protected latch. So, sound asleep, I simply tried slipping through the metal bars.

Although my tiny, first-grade body walked right through with ease, my own screams awakened me when my head got caught between the railings. As I recall, even over forty years later, Daddy was by my side in a matter of seconds.

My father was always a thin man, and didn't exercise or workout. He certainly wasn't muscular. Yet in that moment, his sleepy, scared baby girl was stuck, so he did what he had to in order to *save* me. I remember opening my eyes and seeing his face red and straining, veins protruding from his neck, and his thin arms shaking as he pried the bars apart enough for Mommy and Dawn to pull me into their arms.

You've heard stories of children being trapped in car wrecks, or buried under the debris of a storm. In such situations, against all reasonable explanations, a parent has the strength of a superhero. Against all odds, they literally summon the strength, at a moment's notice, to tear the smashed car door right off the hinges or flip massive amounts of wreckage after a storm in order to save their child. The power of a parent's love is stronger than one's perceived strength.

Over the years that followed, this event was a *go-to story* at parties. I'm not sure which had the biggest impression every time I heard that story, feeling so loved and protected by my father or his smile and laughter every time he told it.

One year, not long before Christmas, my parents had warned me *not* to go into the back room of the basement. Seriously? Didn't they know by the time we were twelve and seven that as soon as you tell a child to *not* do something, they're going to *have* to do it?!

I'll speak for myself on this one. My big sis was the 'good girl'. Dawny always listened and always followed the rules. But as a curious first-grader, I was carefree, adventurous and bold. I knew right from wrong–mostly–and never intentionally did anything to hurt someone. I was also very inquisitive.

After days that felt like months of obeying my parents, my curiosity got the best of me. Everyone else was busy with the day-to-day household chores, and otherwise preoccupied. I snuck downstairs and peered at the forbidden door. I stopped often, frozen in stillness, to listen in case anyone was approaching. The anticipation was thrilling and terrifying at the same time. I reached for the knob on the forbidden door and quickly flung it open, almost as if something may jump out at me, and I needed to be on guard.

I stood in amazement and immediately regretted what I had done. I was shocked and instantly sorry I had disobeyed my parents.

There before me, placed carefully on the workbench, were two big beautiful dollhouses. One yellow and one blue to match our bedrooms.

Daddy had many wonderful attributes but handy-man was not one of them. He was a banker. A number guy. A fashionable, suit and tie type of guy. Yard work on weekends only involved weeding and laying fresh mulch. Realizing he created something so painstakingly built with his own two hands just for *his girls* amazed me. It was obvious, even to me, he attached each piece of the siding and the roof separately. Hand-installed walls separated each room to define the interior almost exactly like our own home. The miniature living room even included tiny couches, end tables, lamps and chairs, all of which matched in color and style. The kitchen had all the essentials for optimal pretending. He also remembered to include a miniature kitchen table, chairs, a fridge and a stove. The upstairs bedrooms were especially similar to our own with beautiful cloth bedspreads and pillows.

His attention to detail was so impressive. I immediately felt overwhelmed with pride, happiness and, of course, guilt. I decided, then and there, that I wouldn't tell a single soul what I had done. My curiosity could ruin his excitement to present his creations to his daughters whom he loved so dearly. Even at seven, I recognized the magnitude of his efforts and vowed to never spoil his fun.

Weeks later, we excitedly ran down the spiral staircase and into the living room to see what 'Santa' brought us. To see those intricately designed, stunning dollhouses in front of our Christmas tree, didn't come as a surprise.

I acted as if I had never laid eyes on them before.

The expression on Daddy's face of happiness and pure joy at our delight was well worth the first secret I ever kept.

But… this was THE moment.

Since the doll houses were from 'Santa' — and the piles of wrapped gifts were from Mommy and Daddy — I realized then for the first time there was no Santa. My parents were Santa. Not as upset as you might expect for a seven-year-old, I felt grateful for how much they always did for us. I certainly didn't want to ruin *their* Christmas fun, so I kept the realization to myself. Another big secret on the weight of my little shoulders. I'll admit, though, it wasn't all selfless. After all, by not letting on that I knew, I would keep getting gifts from Mommy and Daddy *and* Santa… double gifts. Why spoil it for all of us, right?

The State Street home holds countless other vivid memories of my early childhood years.

Lassie, our miniature collie, named by my not-so-original sister, was such a well-behaved, sweet little pup. Mork and Mindy, our goldfish, had a front-row seat to the many 'concerts' on the piano in the living room. It was a big deal for me to feed them every day and watch them swim around. I had wanted fish for the past year, since I started on the swim team, because everyone said I swam like a fish.

I had three aunts, grandparents, a great grandmother, and friends all living on the same street.

This gave me a lot of freedom as a kid. I could roam the street whenever I wanted because I knew trusted loved ones were nearby. It was comforting and reinforced family values. It truly was a wonderful experience.

It's actually amazing how, more than forty years later, so many moments are clear in my mind.

My maternal grandparents, Nonni and Poppop, and my great-grandmother lived right next door. Our double cement driveways were side by side which made it ideal to run around with Lassie, ride bikes and play with friends. Aunt Florence lived in an apartment right above their home. And only a few doors down on the same street, Aunt Mary and Aunt Theresa shared a home.

Those days remain some of the happiest days of my life. Surrounded by family. And as all great Italians do… we ate, yelled, played, loved and laughed. Every day. Not just on holidays.

Later that spring, I remember a specific day when Daddy was working in the yard while I was playing in the driveway.

He took pride in maintaining the yard, and it was one of his weekly hobbies. It was clearly always one of Daddy's favorite things to do, and he was great at it.

For many people, it's just another annoying household chore they put off or hire someone else to do for them. As far back as I could remember, Daddy was always pulling out weeds, refreshing the mulch and planting new azaleas and hostas in his spare time. He took pride in our beautifully landscaped yard and a job well done.

We often saw family and friends outside, especially on weekends. I loved having three of my aunts and my grandparents also living on our very street. On one side were my grandparents and, on the other, the neighbor was a sweet, silver-haired woman. Even though she hunched over a little, I could tell she used to be a tall, thin lady. I remember her talking with my parents often and complimenting me and my sister for a cute shirt or a bow in my hair and always with a sweet smile. She would putter around her yard, not really doing yard work but seemed to be happily busy. I remember overgrown flowering plants and some type of vine growing all over the front of her yard. It seemed messy next to our manicured yard, but I remember thinking it was just as beautiful in its own way.

But on this particular day, she wasn't outside. Daddy was weeding, and I was riding my bike in the driveway. Suddenly, a scream for help startled me, and I just about fell off my bike. I looked up, and Daddy was already running toward the loud cries coming from the silver-haired neighbor's house next door. I ran through our front door to tell Mommy and Dawn. Mommy ran next door to help and told Dawn to bring me over to Nonni and Poppop's house.

Of course I was worried too, and as a little nosey seven-year-old, I wanted to know what happened. Dawn and I waited in the driveway. Minutes later, Mommy came outside and told us the neighbor fell and hit her head. They called the ambulance. I remember her coming out on the stretcher and feeling so sad and worried for her. I noticed my parents talking with her, so it seemed she was okay. I remember thinking she was so old, and I wondered if the nice old lady would recover. Mommy told me and Dawn it was a good thing Daddy was outside and heard her crying for help.

It wasn't life-threatening, and it wasn't earth-shattering enough to make the Daily Journal. But to a little girl who idolizes her father, he certainly seemed like the hero that saved the day.

I loved every part of growing up in a large family with several aunts, uncles and cousins. My mom's parents were the youngest of ten and nine. My dad's father was one of thirteen siblings, and his mother had two sisters that I saw often growing up.

Sundays were for church and family.

Every Sunday we went as a family to morning mass.

After mass, we went to Grandma Panzino's house in Newfield. The second her back door was opened, I could smell her gravy cooking on the stove. Several pots were going at once since my aunts and uncles and at least five of the seven cousins would be arriving shortly.

It was a tiny home on a huge piece of land in Newfield, only about fifteen minutes away. The gray shakers were tattered, and some seemed as though they would fall to the ground with the next light wind. But it was cozy and had its own grandma-esque charm.

As soon as I arrived, being the textbook ornery, youngest child that I was, I immediately went to the old metal cabinet in Grandma's kitchen. It was covered with more than a dozen magnets of various fruits and foods arranged how she liked them. I would rearrange them, sorting them into categories, in my own 'type A' way.

Grandmom would instantly yell…

Gina, no! Not again!

Oh she tried to act mad, as she stood at the stove stirring her gravy. But soon enough everyone laughed including her, and she left the magnets as I arranged them. It was kind of 'our thing'.

My Grandmom Panzino was a little, old Italian woman with a beehive of bright, orange-red hair and often wore red lipstick. She was loud yet loving. She drank her coffee from a percolator on the stove and always had a cigarette in her hand or burning in the tin, ruffled ashtray on a table nearby. The tiny kitchen could barely fit three or four of us at a time. The grownups ate in the kitchen, and the cousins would set up metal TV stands in front of the couch and chair in the adjacent living room.

The TV was never on when the family was there. Elvis was often playing on her little radio. It was a regular station on Sundays, and he was her all-time favorite.

After spaghetti and meatballs, we moved outside, weather permitting, so there was more space for all of us to be together.

Grandmom had an old playhouse in the backyard that all of her grandchildren used over the years. Being the youngest of the cousins, by the time it was my turn, the gray wood structure was cracked and splintered, and the roof seemed a little crooked. I didn't notice back then, and it never prevented me from going inside and "making dinner" for my family with the plastic pots and pans. I'd make everyone come to the window so I could serve them their dinner just as Grandmom did in the house the hour before. Everyone accommodated my imagination and played along.

Beside the playhouse was an amazing vineyard of concord grapes growing around her trellis. I would walk underneath and closely examine each vine, occasionally picking a grape or two as they were my favorite and the best-tasting I'd ever had.

As I scampered around the yard, usually by myself since the cousins and Dawn were anywhere from five to ten years older than me, I was so happy to be surrounded by my family. Grandmom was often lounging in her plastic tri fold beach chaise, especially when her sisters, Aunt Antoinette and Aunt Anne, were there. I can see them in my mind now… one brunette, one blonde and one redhead… three beehives with red lipstick on their big smiles, cigarettes in one hand and a drink in the other, all talking over each other and laughing while Elvis continued to blare through the yard.

Daddy was in his glory. Smiling ear to ear and laughing for what seemed to be hours.

Oh how I miss those days. So many memories with Grandmom Panzino. Sunday afternoon dinners with all the cousins were great, but I also loved when it was 'just us'.

A giant stadium filled with people rushing around with money in hand. Bells and buzzers ringing loudly as Daddy held my hand tightly, and we made our way to our seats. Oh how I loved the excitement at the track with Daddy and Grandmom Panzino.

For an old-fashioned Italian, the only thing equal to family and lots of pasta was playing cards and the horses.

I'm not sure about the rules of today, but back then, kids could go watch the races as long as they didn't go to the window of the betting lines. At some point, I was known as Daddy's good luck charm at those races.

Daddy would say, "Okay, Pooh, pick your horse," as he showed me the choices.

I'd pick based solely on the name I liked the best. I can't explain how, but more often than not, my horse would win.

One time in particular, it must have been a bigger win than usual, I remember me, Daddy and Grandmom jumping up and down and screaming with delight, and hugging me over and over, as my horse crossed the finish line first.

Daddy would grab me and pick me up, kissing my cheek over and over, saying "Atta girl, Pooh."

How wonderful are the memories we shared together. How sweet those early years are to remember those we cherish. It is often the most loving memories that stick out in our minds even all these years later. The feeling of euphoria in the sharing of such happy times with my father is priceless.

Week after week, special moments with both sides of the family brought so much joy to my life. And then, before I knew it, those special weekends came to a screeching halt.

Daddy worked so hard for *his girls* and always wanted to provide all the things he never had as a child. I was about to begin second grade, Dawn heading into high school.

So with another promotion in his banking career and presented with a new business opportunity, we prepared to leave our family and friends and move more than an hour away.

CHAPTER 3

Obsession

Loud buzzers, beeps and whistles blared as children of all ages squealed with delight. Songs by Blondie, Boston, Queen and Michael Jackson blasted through the speakers adding to the fun environment. Children and adults alike burst out into singing or bouncing along to their favorite songs.

It was a typical afternoon at Obsession. Daddy and his friend owned the only arcade in town.

Weeks prior, the exhilaration of planning the new business filled our new home with excitement. Adjusting to the move and beginning at a new school proved difficult at first. I immediately missed my family and friends and the only hometown I've ever known. We all did.

However, the buzz of new experiences on the horizon between Daddy's new role as vice president and the planning of a thrilling new business definitely lessened the shock of the move.

I sat wide-eyed and smiling at the table in our new kitchen. My parents, Dawn and I all painted stacks of quarters, front and back, with Mommy's red nail polish. The anticipation grew as we talked about going after school to use the red quarters at the arcade. Then when Daddy cashed out the machines, he'd set the red quarters aside for us to keep reusing. It was such a fun time for our family and friends.

I watched with enthusiasm and listened closely as Daddy and my sister planned the mural for the wall inside the arcade.

Dawn was inspired by the album cover of her favorite band. She showed Daddy the Boston album and shared her mural ideas. She wanted to paint all the walls dark blue with white stars, like the solar system. In the center, she envisioned a big black, orange, and red spaceship without the guitar. She also wanted the arcade's name on the front of the main spaceship.

They came up with the idea to incorporate that album cover and change it just enough into a regular spaceship with the name of the arcade inside of it.

They agreed that the spaceship idea was brilliant since Space Invaders was so massively popular during that time. One of Dawn's best friends, Pamala, came to see what they were planning and lent a helping hand.

The drop cloths were down, paint cans opened and stirred, and they got down to work. Pam helped paint the planets and rockets surrounding the spaceship with the name of the arcade.

After much consideration, he made a decision. The name of his arcade… OBSESSION. My sister painted the walls with murals of outer space full of stars, planets and spaceships. It was awesome, fun and exciting for young kids with arcades being so popular in the 80s.

My popularity grew quickly–Dawn's too–as more and more classmates from Little Egg Harbor Elementary School and Pinelands Regional High School poured into the arcade after school.

Dawny and I each got a few rolls to play with after school. As Daddy emptied the machines, he'd always set aside the red quarters for *his girls*.

On the slower days, Daddy played with us. He was a big kid and loved playing those games, especially because of his competitive nature. He always tried to beat the high scores. Pac-Man, Space Invaders and Asteroids were among his favorite go-to games.

On busy nights, Dawn and her friend, Jeff, worked for Daddy to help out. Dawn got to wear the change belt filled with quarters. She walked around exchanging bills for coins.

Several nights a week, we'd all go as a family to spend a couple hours at OBSESSION, as long as homework was done first, of course. I remember my mother being in a back room like an office, although at about ten years old, I had no idea nor did I really care about what occupied her time. My only focus was to put my red quarters into Space Invaders and Pac-Man until I ran out. Or until my mother dragged me out of there whining and complaining because it was time for a bath and bed.

"You have school tomorrow, Gina Lynn. Let's go, please."

My response was always the same, "I still have red ones to put in."

I never saw or thought about those esteemed red quarters, after moving back to our hometown.

CHAPTER 4

Tuckerton

As you approached the front porch, stood a large, circular wrought iron rack stacked with firewood. Two chairs and potted plants gave it a homey feel. The stairs and door to the basement on the right and a large, eat-in kitchen a few more steps in to the left. It had a huge island in the middle and a spacious, screened-in porch off the back sliding glass doors. Next to the kitchen table was a large open window framed in dark wood that overlooked the great room.

As you left the kitchen, there was a long hallway raised above the sunken living and formal dining area. The raised catwalk had wood railings, and square wooden pillars beside the steps into the great room. There was a beautiful built-in bookcase at the end of the hallway.

Whoever came to visit had the first time experience with the secret passageway. The bookcase swung open, unexpectedly, with Daddy shouting the unoriginal 'boo' with a huge smile on his face.

It reminded me of the secret wardrobe to enter Narnia as we walked through several coats on either side and stepped into a whole new home. Nonni and Poppop's in-law wing was beyond the bookcase, complete with a master bedroom, full bath, large living room and an eat-in kitchen of their own.

The bookcase prank was one of Daddy's favorites.

Entering back through the bookcase closet and onto the raised catwalk, the wide steps midway down the hall spilled down into the great room.

Being the young performer I was, I especially loved the catwalk. It was the perfect stage for me and Dawn, or my friends and I, to perform for all the other guests.

On the wall of the catwalk was a built-in record player that unfolded from the wall and connected to the intercom system that was installed throughout the home, so when the records spun, we could hear the music all throughout the house. Truly, a wonderful home to host parties.

The impressive, twenty-foot cathedral ceiling displayed dark wood, wall-to-wall planks. The eye-catching living room had a stone fireplace with a raised hearth from the floor to the wooden ceiling. The adjacent dining room fit a dozen people with ease around the solid wood table. There were two sets of sliding glass doors that opened to a cement patio and inground pool, complete with a diving board.

The backyard pool was the party venue for every summer occasion including Memorial Day, birthdays, graduations and the 4th of July to name a few. My parents used the simplest of occasions as an excuse to host friends and family with music blaring from the boom box, tons of food and the constant buzzing of the bug zapper in the background.

The pool was the scene of Mommy and Nonni's near catastrophe one hot summer afternoon.

Neither of them were actually what you would call 'swimmers'. They would stroll around the shallow end squatting gently every so often, but only low enough to dip their shoulders to cool off and careful not to mess their hair. Daddy was expected home from the bank shortly, and it was a good thing. They had only planned on a quick dip before dinner preparations began, until the slip of Nonni's foot.

As they strolled in the cool water in the safe depth of the shallow end, Nonni's foot accidentally hit the slope into the deep end. She instantly slid under the water. Her instinct grabbed onto the nearest object for support, which happened to be my mother. They were giggling and holding each other as they somehow avoided sliding into the deep end. They tried to move closer towards the kiddie side of the pool, but were too busy laughing as they kept slipping near the slope. As if on cue, Daddy walked through the back gate. The splashing and girlie shouting worried Daddy. Slipping and sliding, they were not in real danger yet, but he knew it could go from bad to worse with their uncontrollable laughter causing them to stay off balance.

Mommy recalls hearing Daddy exclaim, *Aw shit!*, as he quickly threw off his suit jacket, diamond watch and shoes before jumping in to 'rescue' the silly ladies.

He escorted them out from the shallow end steps, and they tried to regain their composure. They were fine and still couldn't stop laughing. His suit pants, shirt and tie stuck to his thin frame as he dripped and sloshed onto the patio. They both got 'the look' and that twisted grin before he burst into laughter himself.

The setting of numerous parties and family celebrations, the pool served us well. Kids jumping in off the diving board with belly flops and flips as the moms worried about their hair getting splashed. Music blared throughout the enormous cement patio surrounding three of the four sides. The comical 'Please don't pee in our pool, we don't swim in your toilet' sign hung on the fence perimeter. Several chaise lounge chairs all in a row with umbrellas for the option of shade. The bug-zapper hung in front of the wooden logs wrapped in rope, smartly hiding the pool pump. Faux grass carpeted the area of the patio as guests entered the house through either of the two sets of sliding glass doors. To the left of the patio was a dark wood outside shower in the corner.

My father had an impressive, two-story home built for us based on his own design. His mathematical brain was great at understanding architecture. He often mentioned that he should have been an architect instead of the less-than-stable career in banking.

Daddy thought of every detail and spared no expense to make our new house a home. Not for show but in order to entertain as often as possible as his family and friends were his utmost priority.

It was a small town, and everyone was friendly and welcoming. My parents made fast friends with several couples that Dawn and I referred to as 'Aunt' and 'Uncle' seemingly right away.

There was only one stoplight, an Acme, one bank, one elementary school and one high school. Along the main road, the lake in the center of our new little town was beautiful and lined with giant pine trees. A few impressive homes sat along the water's edge. Around Christmas, a lighted tree would float in the center of the lake and cast a sparkling glow across the surface.

The highlight of the town, for me, was Stewart's Root Beer. It was directly across from the lake, so the view made the experience sitting in the car even better. A visit to Stewart's was one of my personal favorites, after all there wasn't a ton of things to do in our new little town.

Windows half rolled down to hold trays of food and drinks and loud, current music crackling through the outdoor speakers made it fun and exciting for two school kids that never experienced such a 'restaurant'.

Dawny and I sat in the back seat and placed our frosted root beer mugs on the back dash of Daddy's Oldsmobile. The fries were my absolute favorite. Daddy always got his favorite… the root beer ice cream float. We'd talk, laugh and sing along to the music as we enjoyed dinner by the lake.

Driving home after a great time, chatting away already asking about how soon we could go back, I realized I forgot my mug on the back ledge. We were more than halfway home, but before I knew it, we had pulled over to turn back around.

I remember thinking maybe I could keep it as a souvenir, or they could have returned it on our next visit. Instead, Daddy used it as an opportunity to teach another lesson. He didn't label it as such, make a big deal about it or reprimand.

He simply said, "We don't keep things that don't belong to us, even if it was an accident."

It wasn't a lecture, but the fact that he inconvenienced himself and turned around to bring it back spoke volumes to me.

Our new, beautiful home had more than enough space to accommodate friends and family when they came to visit.

Daddy's hard work paid off, and although the transition was difficult at first, things were finally looking up. As the Vice President of Southern Ocean State Bank in Tuckerton and a new business owner,

Daddy seemed happy all of the time. He received a substantial salary increase, and Mommy also worked part-time at my elementary school as a teacher's assistant.

I'll never forget my second grade teacher. As outgoing as I was with family and friends, I was hesitant, and a little nervous, about beginning at a new school in a different town after leaving all my friends in Vineland.

My teacher, we'll call her Mrs. Walker, as I have nothing nice to say, didn't make the transition any easier for me. She was an older, stern woman with brown permed hair. I don't recall her smiling or doing anything fun in her class. Occasionally, they assigned Mommy to work in my second grade class. I was so proud and excited, and I wanted everyone to know she was mine. Mrs. Walker was very nice to Mommy in the classroom, so Mommy just encouraged me to behave and follow directions, and that would surely make her happy. With that in mind, and because my parents raised me to be respectful and kind, my seven-year-old brain thought I could 'cheer her up'. I was so confident that my beautifully-drawn rainbow, flowers and hearts would win her over. I raised my hand and asked if I could give her something. I smiled ear to ear as I handed her my artwork as a gift. She barely acknowledged me, set it down on her desk and told me to go back to my seat. Undoubtedly, I was more than disappointed. To add insult to injury, as I packed to leave during dismissal, I looked back at her to say goodbye with a smile. One more failed attempt to make her happy. I watched as she threw my drawing in the trash.

Sitting at the kitchen table doing homework later that same day, I couldn't stop thinking about why I couldn't make my teacher smile. I followed the rules, raised my hand and never talked during class. Well, okay, I did talk but usually tried to whisper. Daddy came in from work and noticed I was looking sad. When I explained how my picture ended up in the trash, he grew angry and sat next to me

"Pooh, some people act grumpy when something bad has happened to them. I'm sure she didn't mean to upset you," Daddy said. "I know you're a great artist. Just pray for her. Maybe something else makes her sad."

That day I learned that people's actions are more about how *they* feel than they are about *you*. I learned that it is better to show kindness, even without getting anything in return. Yet another lesson learned because of Daddy.

Despite the minor bumps in the road after moving to a new place, there was so much to love about Tuckerton and the nearby shore points.

I loved living in our new town. Our years there were filled with great times, making new friends, day trips out on The Seven Bridges and going to Obsession on nights and weekends to play with my red quarters.

The beaches were full of fun in the sun and great times with family and friends along the water. Little Egg Harbor Township had a road that stretched out over a four-mile peninsula, called The Seven Bridges, towards Brigantine. However, there were only five bridges. It's said that the rough water in that area resulted in the last two bridges not being built.

Most people hung out there on weekends to enjoy the views and go crabbing. Many times we'd bring our family out there, set up the boombox and drop cages off the edge and into the water. Later that night, we'd all enjoy crabs and spaghetti back home.

We sorely missed our friends-like-family from Vineland. And so as it would happen when you miss your loved ones, they inevitably must come for a visit. These wonderful couples have been friends with my parents since before I was born. Everyone had kids around the same time or within a few years apart. My sister, Lisa and Billy were all born within the same year or two. About four to five years later, along came me, Shelly and Lori. With all of our parents being so close, us kids grew up together literally since birth.

Visits when they all came to town were filled with constant laughter, games and music.

My parents' spacious master bedroom was the setting for Lori and I to have a great time. They didn't mind. After all, there was more room to perform our dances there.

With Olivia Newton John spinning on the record player, hairbrush microphones and fancy clothes from Mommy's side of the walk-in closet made for a spectacular show. Even if it was just for the two of us.

Whenever we got tired of dancing, we jumped on the Craftmatic. On the side of the headboard, the remote control to raise the head and foot caught our attention. Excited to give it a try, we grabbed it instead of simply pushing the buttons, and the paint and plaster came off the wall along with the remote.

Worried yet unable to stop laughing, we had a brilliant idea.

We remembered rolls of Christmas wrapping paper tucked in the back of the walk-in when we pulled Mommy's fancy blouses off the hangers for our performance.

In walked Daddy to check into all the ruckus. There beside his headboard, red and green wrapping paper taped onto the wall with a sparkly gold bow and large tag that said, *Do not open until Christmas*.

We figured it would by us some time before he discovered we had a little trouble with the bed remote.

Lori and I got 'the look'. That eye roll and sideways smirk, fighting back his laughter. We knew then we wouldn't be in trouble.

Another 'Vineland Crew' sleepover stands out in my mind. We were having all of our Vineland friends over. Although Tuckerton is only about an hour away, everyone decided to stay overnight. Honestly, they all thoroughly enjoyed one another and were having too much fun to leave.

Three bedrooms were upstairs, so most of us girls roomed together. The other parents and Billy were downstairs on couches and on the floor in the great room.

Early the next morning, my prankster father thought it would be hysterical to sneak down before everyone was awake. He tiptoed quietly into the kitchen to retrieve his weapon of choice. And all of the sudden, the house shook with the crashing and clanging of…

Yep. You guessed it…

Pots and pans!

Yelling ensued as, of course, everyone was awake at that point. Everyone emerged from the other rooms of the house to see what I'm sure they knew was going on. At that point, all I could hear, aside from the clatter, was my father's laughter. One of my best friends, Shelly, called out:

Sammy what are you doing?!

Sammy, oh my God! Stop that!

As they tried to act angry, within minutes, everyone was laughing hysterically.

My memories of our friends are all of fun — the pool, card games, board games, loud music and even louder laughter. Those were some of the best times of my life.

Daddy beamed when he was surrounded by loved ones. His family and friends meant everything to him.

He was a vibrant man. He was always joking around and had a playful and loving personality with his family and friends.

Above all else, Daddy adored *his girls*.

Dawn entered the Miss Teen NJ Pageant along with a couple of her friends from Pinelands. Not because she truly wanted to but because Daddy thought his adorable little *pumpkin* had grown into a beautiful *princess*. Dawn was less than confident during her teen years, so Mommy and Daddy both believed this would help build her confidence and realize how much she had to offer.

Dawn had already proven to be an excellent artist with several accurate sketches, paintings and pottery displayed throughout our home. But after years of dance, they decided dance should be her talent portion of the pageant.

I remember looking up at her from the audience in awe. She wore a beautiful, white organza dress cinched at the waist with a blue satin ribbon and ruffles on the sleeves and hem. Her dark, curly hair was pulled up tightly into a small bun on the top of her head. Red circles painted on her cheeks gave the impression of a mechanical doll. She was 'The Music Box Dancer'. So graceful and en pointe that aspiring dancers like me were impressed with her ability to glide and spin across the huge stage.

Daddy, as usual, beamed with pride. As he watched her perform, the corners of his smile grew wider and wider. He stood up cheering and clapping loudly as she took her bow on stage.

Whether front and center in an audience or stadium emphatically cheering by our side in support of our goals or standing behind us to encourage us to follow our dreams, Daddy was always there for us. He loved us fiercely. Ultimately, his adoration and devotion gave us the courage to follow our own aspirations.

There were a couple drawbacks for young girls growing up under his protective care. We liked boys. Boys came to the house.

Dawn was a junior at Pinelands Regional High School, and everybody loved her. The fact that she was a talented artist, took dance lessons a few times a week and was on the cheerleading squad was the icing on the cake. Deeper than that, she was a true sweetheart, kind and thoughtful, and although arriving in Tuckerton in her seventh grade year when most friend groups had already been established, she made fast friends. Everyone loved her.

She's the firstborn, and on some level, Daddy dreaded this day. He grew concerned and protective and began controlling where she went and who she was with.

On a particular weekend, Dawn's 'friend', Jeff, came to visit at the house. It was about noon, so Mommy started making them *sangwiches* for lunch. They sat on the couch in the living room. Daddy stood in the kitchen, arms crossed, staring at them through the window that opened into the great room. Mommy tried to get him to relax, but he ignored whatever she was saying and kept his eyes on *that boy*. Against her advice, Daddy grabbed the plates and personally delivered lunch. His eyes focused on Jeff with that sideways smirk that Dawn noticed right away.

"Thanks, Daddy."

Dawn quickly grabbed the plates from him and glared at her overbearing father as if to say, *Stop it. Get out.*

He took the cue but returned to the kitchen to spy through the window.

Later that day, about 5pm, another one of Dawn's *friends* paid her a visit. Ironically, his name was also Jeff.

In typical, annoying little sister fashion, I proudly nicknamed her friends *Jeff 12 o'clock* and *Jeff 5 o'clock*.

Daddy was less than thrilled about boys coming to the house to see Dawn. Dreading the idea of his first born approaching the age of dating. This was all new to him. He decided to protect his daughter the only way he knew how.

One evening, my mother heard a noise coming down the hall from their bedroom.

Pssst… Pssst…

It was one of those nights when Dawn had friends over in the great room. Mommy thought she heard something from the hallway outside their bedroom.

PSSSST…

There it was again. It got louder.

She stepped into the hallway and didn't see anyone. Then she heard a frustrated whisper.

"BARB."

Daddy was stomach down, lying head first down the stairs. His toes that had gripped the top step were starting to slip.

She giggled at him, as she often did, and whispered, "What are you doing?!"

"Just help me up!"

He had been peeking through the railing spokes on my sister since 'the boy is right next to her on the couch.'

"You shouldn't spy, hun. Dawn's a good girl."

"It's not her I'm worried about."

He learned his lesson that night. Not to cease his undercover work, but to come up with a new strategy.

Still holding my title of annoying little sister, I teased her relentlessly.

"Who's coming today, Dawny?" I laughed loudly, taking after my father and making jabs, "Jeff 5 o'clock or Jeff 12 o'clock?"

"Sshhh, G, come on. I don't want Daddy hearing you."

Later that night, when Dawn's *friend* came over, Daddy turned to 'the little one' for assistance.

I was a lanky, young girl. Built like my father. And all too excited to help him execute his new plan. The new idea was for me to go head first down the stairs while he held my skinny ankles. I used the opportunity to make some extra cash. After all, I was saving for the new Barbie convertible. Daddy promised a quarter for every new piece of information. It was our secret. Now that I was an accomplice, I couldn't ruin it by telling my sister what we were up to.

"They're watching TV," I reported.

"That's it? Are they both on the couch?"

Naively, I retorted, "Of course they're both on the couch, Daddy. How else would he be able to put his arm around her like that? Hmf."

Needless to say, he was less than thrilled and lowered me back down to keep watching. I made a whole pack of quarters that night! Daddy said we could paint them red tomorrow to use at Obsession.

Our scheme didn't last long. Nothing juicy ever took place. Mommy was right. Dawn was a good girl and, in my eight-year-old opinion, boring and simply enjoyed hanging out with her friends and watching tv.

Daddy was always having a good time, and he was a good practical joker. In a mostly innocent, playful manner. It was all in good fun. He was harmless. Although if you asked his friends, the usual targets, they may disagree.

There was a huge, vacant corner lot only a block from our house where all the neighborhood kids played wiffle ball or football. Riding my bike from house to house and playing in the woods that led to a friend's house on the next road over was almost a daily occurrence.

After a rough second grade at Little Egg Harbor Township Elementary School, my parents, along with several other families, arranged for busing from Tuckerton to Pomona.

Up until that point, Dawn and I had always attended Catholic school. My parents thought it would help me adjust better.

The lengthy, bumping bus ride every day was miserable for us all. The nuns and daily mass did provide a familiarity for a little girl missing home, but by the end of the year, all of the families felt the trip alone just wasn't worth it.

Luckily for me, I returned to Little Egg Harbor. The next three years included fantastic teachers and lifelong friends. It was so enjoyable, and I finally started to love school.

Watching Mrs. Hoffman as she strolled to the front of the classroom with her shiny dark hair of considerable length swishing behind her, I immediately was intrigued. My Italian, frizzy curls never swished. She was as informative and calm as she was attractive and kind.

"Your penmanship is beautiful, Gina," was all I needed to hear. The more she praised me, the more my smile grew as my little hands wrote as much as I could imagine.

In the fifth grade, Mrs. Spooner developed and encouraged my writing more than anyone up until that point in my young life. A fresh, crisp journal placed in front of me on my desk filled me with a new found excitement for school. It was my very own journal.

I'd written in my own diaries for years. During that time, I used a light blue, Holly Hobby hardcover at home. It even had a lock and miniature key in which to hide away my secrets and dreams. All of my stories were just between me, myself and I written privately in my bedroom. Until now.

Writing for other people was new to me. Even if it was just for the teacher's eyes, it felt important and special to me.

Every morning, I eagerly entered the classroom to see a new quote had appeared on the chalkboard. I had the pleasure of writing what I thought about the phrase and explaining what it meant to me. I was one of few students to respond with more than a sentence or two. Most days I filled the page with my ideas, often two pages. Mrs. Spooner wrote in the margins agreeing with, or even complimenting, my eyes.

That was when I officially became a writer at heart. I was hooked and thanks to her initial support and encouragement, I still write every day.

In walked a little Italian girl with a great big smile chatting and laughing with other students. She caught my eye.

"I know you. Hi Gina! You were in Spooner's class last year."

Our classes switched for reading and math groups. We met then, along with many other great new friends.

"Yeah, hi Melissa."

"I'm excited for sixth with Mr. Deyo this year. I heard he's great."

Melissa and I stayed after school for the Stamp Club with Mr. Deyo. To us, he was great at everything. Laughter filled weekends, splashing around in the pool, class trips to Great Adventure were just a few of the wonderful memories we created together.

Most of my countless fun-filled days by the sixth grade were either at the Romano household or at the Panzino Pool Parties. Melissa and I were regular pen pals since the day we left and have been best friends to this very day.

My family loved our life in Tuckerton. The friends we made during those five years were people we almost instantly considered family. Mommy and Daddy built very close bonds with other couples. They all had children around the same age as Dawn and me. Most of my childhood memories in Tuckerton involved wonderful times with the O'Neills, DiGuilios and Vilardis. Countless fun-filled gatherings filled with laughter made our years in Tuckerton truly enjoyable. We were with our amazing friends for every birthday party, pool party, holiday celebration and sports event.

I sat with my legs crossed on the floor in the living room. A plate full of hard-boiled eggs, hot dogs and macaroni salad on the wooden coffee table in front of the TV. The chaos ensued as I watched and listened to the war of words.

Daddy especially loved watching football on Sunday at the O'Neills' so he could tease Aunt Flo about the Eagles. They were die-hard fans, so games against his adored Cowboys were most electrifying. Aunt Flo never backed down. As they debated the ability of the players and the outcome of the game, they both smiled through their 'arguments'.

You don't encounter people that have your back, make you laugh, hold you when you're sad and bring true joy to your life that often, but when you do, it's truly a blessing. Those amazing people were, and still are, family.

Yet, after a few years, the first setback occurred for my family.

My father sat with his head in his hands, not realizing I was about to walk into the great room. I was only about ten, but I knew something was very wrong. After all, it was the middle of the day, and he wasn't at the bank.

My mind raced from one thought to the next within seconds, trying to figure out what was wrong. I wondered if he was fighting a cold but knew that wouldn't stop him from going to work. I thought maybe he had a fever, but he wasn't in bed or even laying down. Then, Mommy caught me watching him and whispered.

"Go give him a hug, Pooh."

"What's wrong with him, Mommy? Is he okay?"

"He had a rough morning at work, but he'll be better quickly, after a hug from his Pooh bear."

She didn't have to tell me twice or convince me. I worshiped my Daddy. We all did. I swiftly pranced down the catwalk and leapt down the stairs calling out to him.

"Hi, Daddy! It's me."

"Hey there, Pooh. Whatcha up to?"

He wiped his face with his hands and summoned up a forced smile, which was proof of just how upset he really was. I didn't take it personally but felt worried about why he was so distraught. I made it my mission to cheer him up. I had never seen him like this in all of my ten years.

Sal was known as a man of great integrity at the bank. His attention to detail and astute knowledge of numbers made him very good as VP. Every employee at the bank appreciated the fact that he was so approachable and willing to listen to each person. But even more than that, he was kind and quick to tease or crack a joke, which kept everyone smiling and happy at work.

The customers knew him as a friendly advisor. He was a thorough man with attention to detail. They appreciated how he clearly explained their options with honesty and patience. He helped so many hardworking people to secure a loan from the bank which enabled families to better their own lives. Daddy was humbled for the opportunity to help others. Customers knew they could trust him.

Saddened by what he'd heard, Daddy sat and listened intently to his customers. One after another pleaded with him for help. He believed in people. He gave everyone the benefit of the doubt. He was quick to befriend everyone he came across. But now, he was faced with a decision. He knew what was right, and after hearing their stories, the torment of his hard-working clients, he knew he had to take action and confront his friend.

Bursting into the corner office was unlike him. The president was smug and sat with a sly grin.

"Have a seat, Sal. Calm down. Let's talk."

"I will not sit down. How could you take advantage of these people? Kickback in order to approve their loans?! It's unethically and legally wrong," Daddy stammered.

"I won't leave you out, Sal. You can get in on the action too."

"I will not. And I will not let you take advantage of these hard-working, good people."

"Let me warn you, Sal," as the president finally stood from his chair, pointing his finger sternly, "If I go down, you're going down with me."

Daddy gave a look of disgust and turned sharply, storming out of the office. He immediately reported the illegal activity to the board, and the investigation began.

Soon after the confrontation, Daddy fell ill. He was in a great deal of pain, and it was determined by his doctors that he had a hernia. He would have to take some sick time. He was worried about his customers and the investigation. Daddy rarely missed work, but it had to be taken care of. He would need to slow down and get the rest his body needed to recover properly.

During Daddy's illness, the bank president took advantage of his absence and continued his business as usual. That's when he sealed his own fate.

During the investigation, loan approvals 'signed by Daddy' were dated during the same time he was out sick, and a couple of them had the actual date of his hernia surgery. That was the proof that ultimately cleared his name.

As a man who took pride in his solid character of truth and dedication to all that is fair and just, he was beyond heartbroken that anyone would think for a second he was involved in anything illegal. He was crushed that even a few members of the board doubted his integrity. He was an honest, good man. Everyone knew this as a fact. His Christian beliefs and kind heart understood that they were just doing their jobs.

Daddy entered the board room and saw all twelve members seated at the long, cherry wood table. He smiled as he entered the room, pulling the door closed behind him, and sat alone across from the other suits.

His heart raced as they summarized the reason they were meeting. He listened without saying a word as they spewed terrible terms such as *embezzlement*, *lies* and *investigation*. Knowing, of course, that he was in no way a part of the story they divulged, he continued to listen in silence. The board president explained to Daddy that the votes were in his favor, and they determined he was innocent.

After respectfully listening to their results, he stood up and spoke for the first time in that meeting. With pain in his eyes, he spoke calmly and gave his resignation. He explained that his good character and ethics are the fiber of his being, and although he understood that the investigation was required in a situation such as this, the fact that some of them doubted his morality was too hurtful to accept.

He smiled, shook each hand and walked out with his head held high.

Determined to find a new job as fast as possible, Daddy was open to the idea of leaving banking all together. Before we knew it, he was on to a new exciting opportunity.

Playing cards is in our nature. As far back as I can remember, it was one of our favorite pass times. Daddy taught me many card games over the years.

Leaning on the green felt pool table in our basement, Daddy practiced dealing. Dawn and I were excited, and just happy as usual, to be playing a game with our Daddy. He taught us blackjack and explained that he'd be working at Harrah's Casino in Atlantic City.

It was exciting and fun for him at first. He even had the thrill of meeting Gladys Knight & the Pips one evening at his blackjack table. But the night shift proved too difficult for a family man like Daddy. He started missing out on dinners, events and even a couple activities for *his girls*. That was unacceptable to him.

Dawn and I adjusted well to life in Tuckerton. We all loved it there to be honest. Dawn especially enjoyed her high school life and the close friendships she created over the years. Not willing to return to the same bank after the loan debacle and no longer willing to give up family time with his girls, he had accepted a manager, loan officer position at a bank back home.

"Daddy just got a new job, a better job. A job that will let me see you, Dawn and Mommy a lot more like it used to be. How would you feel about moving back to Vineland, Pooh?"

CHAPTER 5

Coming Home

One sweltering hot sunny summer day, I strolled down the street in my bikini, without a care in the world. It was a beautiful, middle-class, quiet neighborhood with perfectly manicured yards and well-kept homes of typical middle-class families. The neighborhood pool club was only four houses down from our home. A short walk.

Summer days bring freedom for most teens with working parents. Laying by the neighborhood pool baking in the sun with music blaring on the boom box and hanging with friends was an everyday occurrence at the Franklin Heights pool. Laps back and forth, racing for the prize of 'I'm the best swimmer' and waiting for the cute boy you're crushing on to throw you in the deep end to confirm his mutual attraction were the highlights of summer.

Except in my case, I never truly had freedom.

I was blessed to always have my grandparents live down the street, next door or actually with us in their attached 'in-law wing' of our home.

Summer days at the pool down the street were fun for sure. However, one day I made a crucial mistake in the eyes of my loving and protective grandparents.

Oh sure, it's all fun and games until the little Italian-Catholic girl gets snagged by her old-school, strict poppop driving past.

Although I, personally, saw nothing wrong with my actions, the absolute horror and disapproval Poppop displayed didn't come as too much of a surprise considering his old-fashioned, and to my mind, outdated viewpoint. Raised to respect my parents and grandparents, I silently endured the verbal lashing and followed his command to quickly get into the car before 'God forbid someone sees you!' I swore to myself I'd use my coverup from now on if only to avoid the embarrassment of being forced into the car only to drive three houses down.

Our close-knit family wasn't all bad. As a matter of fact, even as a teenager, I always felt grateful for the enjoyable, fun times spent together. Sure, holidays and celebrations were of great importance, but it was the day-to-day living that provided both security and a sense of pride and happiness. Of course we had our challenges and tiffs from time to time just like everyone else I'm sure. But for the most part, we genuinely appreciated one another.

Growing up, I often saw Mommy going out of her way to cater to Daddy, a common scenario in traditional Italian-Catholic households of the 70s and 80s. Yet it was clear she took genuine delight in pleasing him. Daddy, in turn, showed equal appreciation for her efforts to serve him.

I watched every morning for many years as she added three sugars and whole milk to his large mug of coffee. She'd walk down the hallway to bring it to him in their bedroom as he got ready for another stressful day at the bank. When I was a teenager, I insisted on serving Daddy his coffee each morning just to see his big smile and hear his 'thanks Pooh' with a kiss on my cheek.

When you are blessed with a person who will bend over backwards just to make you smile, who will inconvenience themselves to support your endeavors, you also then want to do anything to return the love and show your appreciation.

One of the many ways Daddy showed his love for us was at Christmas. He was all about Christmas from making a list for each person to the shopping itself. From the music and the decorations to the fact that each person had to have their own special wrapping paper so all their presents matched one another and also matched the beautiful decorations on the tree.

Displayed proudly in the corner, carefully placed on a wooden stand to raise it all the way to the ceiling, he stunning Christmas tree was covered in mauve and cream. With great attention to detail, brilliant golden ribbons were delicately tied around every ornament and placed with utmost care. The ornaments purposely coordinated with the mauve, cream and baby blue 80s decor of the living room. The stained, off-white dress trimmed with lace flowed down from the angel atop the highest branch.

Just like every year, I can remember the holiday carols of Neil Diamond, Barbra Streisand, Frank Sinatra, and Dean Martin echoing in our home. Christmas 1985 was like all the other Christmases - a joyful and spectacular time for the family.

A couple years later, I was sitting in the audience with friends and family. One of my best friends on stage as a contestant in the county pageant.

Lori was accurately performing a dance I had choreographed. After weeks of me playing the role of 'hard-core instructor', she, knowing me as she did, was less than impressed with my skill and knowledge of the art and voiced her annoyance on more than one occasion.

I laugh at the memory now, knowing that we were a lot alike.

Lori and I took dance lessons for years together at The Arts of Dance Center in our hometown. We both enjoyed it from the beginning, but after I became a dance instructor at our studio and a lead performer with the local dance company, I gained the reputation as 'a dancer'.

Choreography became my latest passion. Which may explain, partly, why I was so invested in her performance. I felt like a mama bird watching her baby fly from the nest.

Lori's performance made me so proud. She executed every move just how I envisioned it. I was so happy for her and felt confident that her performance would definitely increase her chances of winning.

I applauded and beamed with pride. I remember her looking so beautiful and poised on stage. The roar of the applause made me wish it was me on that stage, but my happiness for her accomplishment quickly took over.

Frank and Lynn, Lori's parents, along with Lisa, her sister, were fiercely clapping their hands. My father cheered so loudly some would think it was *his* daughter on stage.

My father was just as proud of Lori the night of the Junior Miss Cumberland County pageant as he was of me for being the choreographer. He cared for his best friends' children as if they were his own. Daddy was front and center in the audience that night, just as he always was for me and Dawn.

It was the end of the pageant, and they were about to announce the runners-up and crown the new Junior Miss. We sat on the edge of our seats with anticipation. By the time they got to the first runner-up and Lori's name hadn't yet been called, we felt confident she would soon be crowned.

But then, as they announced the winner they said another contestant's number along with announcing Lori's name.

The crowd all stammered and started calling out and questioning the judges in confusion.

Just then, my father stands up to join in the calamity and shouts, "She won fair and square!"

Polite, respectful and probably embarrassed Lynn, who adored my father and knew how much he loved her daughter, quickly demanded, "Sammy, sit down!"

As it turned out, Daddy was right. After the judges double-checked their scorecards, they announced and crowned my best friend Junior Miss Cumberland County 1986!

Daddy was the type of man who loved his nieces, nephews, cousins and his friends' children as if they were his own. He just had so much love to give.

He looked forward to welcoming the next generation. He often talked to me and Dawn about having grandchildren. He couldn't wait. Deeply invested in those he loved, he was generous to all.

So when Frank and Lynn had their third child, a son, Daddy was so excited. He went to visit little

Frankie with a gift. Daddy's face lit up with such happiness, Lynn recalls, as he gave him a big Mickey Mouse pillow, which they still have to this day.

Many years later, their oldest child, Lisa, had her first son, Dominick. Daddy, once again, was all too excited to visit and bring him a gift.

Daddy grinned from ear to ear as he handed him a teddy bear night light with a Dallas Cowboys hat and shirt on. He knew, of course, that his friends were all Philadelphia fans, but that was the jokester in him they all loved. Lisa laughed and gave Daddy a hug in appreciation. She saw his excitement and knew he had such a huge heart.

One of the attributes people loved about him the most was his fun-loving humor and innocent teasing. He was always smiling and laughing, enjoying the company of those he loved the most.

In the spirit of that humor, as Daddy loved to tease and joke around, I followed his lead. As handsome as he was, he had very full, dark eyebrows that, to me and Dawn, were an easy target. He was meticulous about getting his hair just right, wearing his gold jewelry and never forgetting his cologne. Even in shorts and a tank top, or his favorite Dallas t-shirt, he always looked put together and fashionable.

One day I noticed his eyebrows were lacking the usual manicure. Now was my chance to tease back, and, more importantly, get a laugh out of him. In the middle of a conversation, I slowly brought my bent finger in between my own eyebrows with a smirk on my face. As my eyes focused on his own eyebrows, almost about to laugh, he picked up on what I was teasing about. Those bushy eyebrows in no way took away from that handsome face. We all knew it, including him. He quickly tried smoothing the hairs above his deep brown eyes, laughing hysterically.

Gotcha, Daddy!

From that day on it became a go-to tease to get back at him for whatever joke he was attempting or during those times he needed a good laugh.

It was those little things. The moments in life that build connection and affection within a relationship. The inside joke that always brought a smile to our faces. He was such fun. Easy to talk to, approachable and loving.

His steadfast love served me well throughout my teen and young adult years, as well.

My high school years brought extremely busy schedules with endless activities for which my parents were responsible. They were my personal taxi almost every day of the week.

As a parent now myself, I understand the chaos and self-sacrifice it requires to encourage and support your children in multiple activities.

I was in the Spirit Club, cheerleading, select choir, school plays, Key Club, and I was the secretary of the Italian Club. I also danced every night after school.

My father was happy to oblige, dropping me off and picking me up day after day to support every endeavor.

But the idea of his little girl dating threw him into protective mode as he dreamed up new ways to safeguard 'the little one'.

His Italian-Catholic view of boys dating his daughters is a classic. These poor kids had to come into the house and sit on the couch opposite my father as the myriad of questions ensued.

I hid down the hallway with my mother holding my hand in support. We tried to whisper so they wouldn't hear us as we eavesdropped. Inevitably, we'd get the giggles.

I suppose a typical teenage girl would be embarrassed, but it only made me feel safe, loved, and protected.

Mommy and I stifled our laughter as Daddy fired away.

What's your last name?

Who are your parents?

Do you get good grades?

Do you play sports?

Where are you taking my daughter?

What are your intentions?

What time will you be bringing her home?

If at any point, he didn't like their response, he'd calmly say, *you can go now, she's staying here.*

I thought to myself about the boy on the couch.

Why does he endure the interrogation? How can he sit there so calmly?

Getting into his car, I'd wave to Daddy as he watched us pull away. Surprisingly, the boy would say, "Your dad is awesome!"

He was a great father, and it was evident that he had a genuine spirit and just wanted to protect his little girl. His old-fashioned, traditional and loving ways made him a little overprotective, but the good guys didn't mind. It actually cultivated respect, and many of them developed friendships with him over the years, even after we stopped seeing each other.

Once Daddy gave his approval, he fully embraced the person and treated them like family. He established close bonds and demonstrated affection and care towards all of mine and Dawn's friends. He treated them as though they were his own kids. We often attended parties, went out to dinner and even had double dates with our parents. Merighi's Savoy Inn was where our parents and friends would meet up to celebrate New Year's Eve. Our family had a long-standing friendship with the Merighis, and my father was always committed to supporting local businesses, especially when friends were the owners.

One particular New Year's Eve bash, we were all on the dance floor more than at our tables which wasn't uncommon. Daddy danced with Lene, one of Dawn's best friends, because after all, she was like another daughter to him. The funny thing is, Lene doesn't dance. But because it was Dad Panzino she wasn't about to refuse.

I especially loved to dance. It was one of the few things that kept me out of trouble, in those days.

I was not the easiest teenager, especially compared to my sister Dawn. She always followed the rules. She was respectful and listened to everything my parents said, whether she liked it or not.

I, on the other hand, was more spirited. I always voiced my opinion and would disagree often. I was headstrong and convinced that I was old enough to make my own decisions. When we disagreed, there was often an argument, especially between me and my mother.

Being a mother now looking back, she always had valid points. Although when you're seventeen and feeling like an adult but being treated as a child, you don't always see it that way.

Frustrated with the unfair rules, I had enough and packed my things. A change of clothes, toothbrush, blow dryer and hair brush thrown into the small suitcase.

I thought about the last time I used that suitcase. I was in Florida with my parents and Dawn visiting Nonni and Poppop. They went for the winters, and we'd always visit because we missed them so badly.

Okay, yeah, I have a great family. But I'm grown up, and they can't keep treating me like a child!

I quietly dropped it out of the back window of my bedroom. There was no point in having another big argument. The plan was when everyone was asleep, I would go outside, get my suitcase, get into my car and drive off.

I didn't plan to go far. Aunt Mary's was the best option.

She was my godmother, Daddy's sister. We got very close as I got older, and she was a great listener. She spoke to me as though I was an adult. I could complain to her about how unfair they were and how they treated me like a child.

I went about the evening as if nothing was any different. Sitting on the couch as Daddy ate his Tastykake Krimpets watching his Dallas Cowboys and chit-chatting with my mom. I was acting as natural as can be when off in my peripheral vision I noticed something on the floor in the dining room.

He realized I noticed, and immediately, a huge grin developed across his thin, handsome face. My head snapped back at him as I noticed it was my suitcase.

Yes, the same one that I so cleverly dropped out of my bedroom window thinking I outsmarted my father.

He was sitting there, calm as could be, chatting with me as if nothing was going on. I looked at him trying to be angry and holding in my laughter.

He's good…

I stomped over to the suitcase, grabbed it aggressively and stomped down the hall to my bedroom.

He couldn't help himself, and I heard him break out in laughter.

As I write this today, I'm not sure what I was trying to run away from. I was blessed with involved parents that always cared and had my best interests at heart. They were present at every event and performance. They always wanted to give me and my sister everything they never had. They were patient, kind and supportive.

It's not that I wanted to leave my parents. I was just trying to forge my own path of independence. I just wanted to be treated like the adult I was becoming.

What happened next reminded me how much I truly enjoyed and appreciated my family.

This day was not very different from most. The kitchen is filled with family. Daddy, Mommy, Aunt Mary, Grandmom Panzino and Dawn. I brought the boom box out from my bedroom and placed it on the kitchen counter. Roxette was blasting "The Look", and I started dancing around the kitchen, which wasn't uncommon.

I was teasing Daddy about his hair, explaining that he was getting older and it should be styled differently, as I ran my fingers over his head. Daddy rolled his eyes at me, allowing me to 'fix it' and started laughing. I ran down the hall and returned with my hair mousse and hair brush. Draped a towel over his shoulders right there in the kitchen, on display for the rest of the family. I added a huge dollop of product and started combing in a more flattering style. Playing to the crowd, as a performer does, I broke away from his styling chair and took the spotlight, showing off my dance moves and singing in my hairbrush.

She's got the look... she's got the look...

Daddy just looked at me, as he always did, with that big smile. Everyone was clapping and laughing. I pointed my hairbrush mic at Daddy, and he willingly played along.

...and I go la la la la la...

Times like that, filled with laughter and the unexpected joys, reminded me of just how blessed I was.

Fun and games aside, performing was my driving force by the time I was a senior in high school.

My days consisted of teaching dance to three-to-seven-year-olds after a day of algebra, English and drama classes. Despite the fact that I was in the select choir, the secretary of the Italian club, a member of the Key Club and a varsity cheerleader, my true love was dance.

My father was not only supportive and proud but always present. You could always find him front and center at every game, performance and activity. He was easily recognized with a huge smile on his tanned face cheering like the loud-mouth, proud Italian father he was. His devotion and loyalty to family and friends were one of the attributes people admired about him the most, including me.

I learned that from him.

Loyalty and love was like a silent mantra that reverberated throughout my being since I can remember because of his example.

Daddy was loved and respected by everyone who knew him.

Dozens of family and dear friends filled the house with excitement and laughter. The side tables and hearth were lined with gifts in the den. Decorations were all over the house as everyone joined together to celebrate Daddy. We felt confident that we were able to pull off the surprise for his fiftieth birthday. Aunt Dottie and Uncle Ronnie graciously offered their home for our special event. Friends and family arrived from out of town, some driving from more than an hour away to celebrate a wonderful man. Everyone was dressed up, with drinks in hand, and happily planning for his arrival at any moment.

That fall, I started college.

I was a dance major at Glassboro State College, only thirty minutes from home. Daddy loved the proximity and encouraged me to live at home and commute each day. I happily agreed. Not only did it save them money, but I could enjoy the home cooked meals and looked forward to the time enjoying my family and friends.

After dancing my whole life, that was all I could think about doing and all I ever wanted to do. It seemed like the natural progression, after all my years performing on stages, to major in dance.

My dream was Broadway or a huge, off-stage performance in Philadelphia or amusement parks. I went to auditions for Disney, Busch Gardens Virginia, Kings Dominion and a couple productions in Philly.

My father was always so proud of me and encouraged my dreams.

For almost fifteen years, he paid for countless lessons. Week after week. Month after month. Year after year. My parents spent their hard-earned money on innumerous dance costumes for recitals and performances over the years.

I wasn't really sure what I was going to do with a major in dance, but at the time, that's all I wanted. And, as always, Daddy was front and center cheering and clapping loudly at every performance.

A year later, the dance program was phasing out because they didn't have enough students in the major. I wasn't ready to stop dancing, so I decided to audition for the Towson State University dance program in

Maryland. I was accepted for the upcoming fall semester based on my dance audition.

Mommy and Daddy drove me to Maryland–always there for me–to help me move into to my new dorm and to meet my roommate. Juggling a cart packed with suitcases, boxes and bins, we stuffed everything into the elevator. With no room left for my parents, Daddy said they'd follow behind when the next elevator became available.

Suddenly, the elevator jolted causing me to bounce before coming to an abrupt stop. I panicked and yelled for my Daddy.

"Daddy, help me! Where are you?"

"I'm right here, Pooh. Are you okay?"

"No, I'm stuck. Get me out of here!"

What was I thinking leaving my home? I can't believe this is happening. It's going to break and plummet me into the basement. I can't breathe. It's too small in here. I need to go home.

"I called maintenance, Pooh. They'll be right here."

"Daddy, don't leave me."

Just as I started to cry, now believing I should have never left home and this was surely a sign to go home with my parents, I felt a slight bounce in the elevator and then a smooth ride to my dorm floor. The doors opened, and Daddy stood there with open arms to greet me. Holding back his laughter, he reaffirmed everything was fine.

Meeting my roommate and having my parents helping me unpack and settle in helped to ease my nerves, I grew more and more excited to be on my own and having a sweet and kind roommate. I realized I may have overreacted just a bit over the elevator incident and felt ready for them to return home to New Jersey.

Now calm and happy to be on campus, I walked the ground to explore.

The beautiful maple and oak trees towered above me. Their branches reached up towards the sky and provided shade as I walked through the perfectly manicured paths. I smiled as I inhaled deeply, excited to be on my own on such a beautiful campus. The delightful smell caused me to follow the scent. Huge trees with heart-shaped leaves and light purple flowers were just up the hill and around the bend. As I walked along the beautiful paved paths that traversed many hills throughout the campus, I was filled with excitement of living here and dreamed of success in the new dance program with the opportunity of performing on a bigger stage.

I was on my own, more than three hours away from my parents and family, in Vineland, NJ. I was relieved to have a great roommate, friendly and kind.

Jessica was as smart as she was beautiful. She came from a loving, Christian family that I could relate to, and they lived nearby in Maryland. I was invited to go home with her a couple weekends.

Jessica sat at the piano after family dinner. She was almost too perfect. Talented, smart, kind and beautiful. I felt like I won the roommate lottery. We shared many laughs and encouraged each other throughout that first year together in the dorm. It was thanks to her that I made fast friends and worried much less about being away from home.

The writer in me loved to jot down all of my day-to-day activities in letters and send them home to my parents and friends. The thrill of getting mail brought me to the mail room almost every week.

I was reminded of the time Dawn went on a church retreat. It was during highschool, so it was her first time away from home. Daddy would have never allowed *his girls* to go away without him, but since it was the youth group from church, he made an exception. My parents and I wrote her letters while she was away. Daddy always wrote his own special letter to *his girl*. We continued writing to her when she later went to college even though she was only thirty minutes away at Glassboro State. I was filled with excitement for Dawny, knowing she would appreciate the letter. It was so heartwarming and special that I already looked forward to my own letters from home when I was old enough to go away.

It was no different when it was my turn. The letters from my parents always brightened my day. Daddy wrote his own section after Mommy's paragraphs stating how much she missed her little girl. Daddy wrote his own thoughts separately, reminding me of how proud he was of my accomplishments as a dancer in the Towson program.

Daddy provided me with a generous allowance on a credit card I was able to use on campus, but I couldn't, in good conscience, allow him to pay for my frivolous spending on pizza, fresh baked goods and homemade ice cream to enjoy with my friends from the campus cafeteria. The 'freshman fifteen' was no joke, even though I was a sophomore, and the grueling ballet classes were no match for the chocolate chip cookies.

I needed my own spending money. I started working as a dreaded telemarketer for MBNA selling credit cards. Needless to say, working on commission, both my parents, grandparents and my sister sat through my script over the phone and signed up for their own cards to show their support, as usual.

I sat in a sad, tiny cubicle in a room full of 200 people, each of them in their own depressing 'offices' which were more like boxes made from walls of felt. Making cold calls for hours, unsuccessfully trying to get people to sign up for the credit card, was a miserable four hours for five nights a week.

I always took a cab back to the dorm since I didn't have my car on campus. I arrived back late one evening and was taken by surprise.

I always had my keys in hand approaching my building, until this night. I was disappointed in my job performance and worried about not having enough money in my next paycheck. As I fumbled in the dark looking for the key to unlock the dormitory entrance, next thing I knew, my arms were pinned behind my back, and my forehead hit my knees. I heard two deep male voices barking orders at each other to search my pocketbook and wallet. I wondered what would happen when they realized I have no money and nothing of value to steal.

Just then, one of the guys stood in front of me, and as I looked up, I only caught a glimpse of his face before he struck the side of mine. I was shoved to the ground, chin to the pavement. As I looked out into the shadows towards the running footsteps, all I could see was two men in dark hoodies running away up the hill.

I layed on the pavement alone, late at night, trying to make sense of something horrific. I thought of Daddy and worried about what he would say and do.

Needless to say, the phone call to my father was his worst nightmare. He didn't want me to go to Maryland. Truth be told, he never wanted me to leave Vineland if he had it his way. And he certainly never wanted his baby girl more than three hours away, all alone on campus. I don't know how he did it but that night, he arrived at my dorm in two and a half hours. He sat by my side and listened as I told the RA and the campus police the story for the third time. He fought back tears and seemed to be shaking. He didn't say a word. He just stared at the floor and listened intently, his hand gently rested on my back.

It was useless to explain to the sketch artist what I saw for the two seconds in the dark before I hit the ground. Obviously, they couldn't figure out who did it and resolved that it was just college kids after a few extra bucks.

Driving back from the police station, Daddy still didn't speak as he squeezed my hand into his. We drove to my dorm room, and Daddy helped me pack all of my things that very night. He had just about enough of me being so far away and alone. We loaded my belongings into Daddy's car and headed home. I never went back.

I can only imagine the anguish he felt. He was so calm it worried me. Clearly, he was devastated but tried to remain calm so as not to upset me any further. After a few miles of barely talking, he asked if anything else happened besides them roughing me up. I knew what he meant, and my heart broke knowing he was terrified of my response.

No, Daddy. They didn't do anything else. I'm okay. Really, I am. I'm happy to be going home. Now you can keep a closer eye on me, the way you like.

He let out an audible sigh of relief. Of course, the thought of two men grabbing and smacking his little girl was horrible in its own right. I know he thought it definitely could have been worse. We talked on the way home about how grateful we were that it wasn't more serious. We even started to laugh and joke about how he was thrilled I was moving back home 'where I belonged'.

I was filled with gratitude for my Daddy. Driving so late at night to rescue his Pooh bear and holding it together as not to upset me. As always, he was right there by my side doing all he could for me.

So by the time I returned home to Vineland, the dance program had already dissolved at Glassboro. It was renamed Rowan University. I started the very next semester in the closest field to dance I could get. My new major was Health and Exercise Science. I was always an athlete whether it was dance, track or swimming, so going to school to become a physical education teacher was the next best thing.

I loved that program! All my classes were amazing: weightlifting, tennis, physiology, anatomy and kinesiology. It was fantastic. I was thoroughly enjoying college again and looked forward to all of my classes. I commuted from Vineland each day and started waitressing part time, only miles from home. Daddy was thrilled.

Three years later, I graduated with a 4.0 GPA and passed an additional praxis exam to become a classroom teacher. The following September, the next town over hired me and I started my full-time teaching career under contract at twenty-five years old. I still lived at home just how Daddy liked it. But not for long.

Going to lunch mid-work week with his daughter's boyfriend was a little suspicious. Daddy sat across from Gene, knowing why they were there. He knew Daddy well enough to do this with honor and respect for Daddy. By that point, Gene was already part of the family, so he was used to the teasing. Daddy stretched out lunch as long as he could, smirking and cracking jokes to prevent him from asking the question.

Finally, he placed the small box next to Daddy's sandwich plate. Daddy smiled from ear to ear and cracked another joke about Gene not being 'his type'. They laughed, and he ultimately got Daddy's permission with a big hug and man-pat on his back

Standing at the back of Sacred Heart Church with Daddy, he faced me and placed his hands on each arm. I'm sure the thought of emptying his bank account for a wedding fit for a princess crossed his mind. Yet, he looked me in the eye and calmly spoke with a smile.

"Pooh, we can go right, or left…" Motioning out the back door with his head.

"Daddy, I'm getting married today."

And with that, he squeezed my arms as if he never wanted to let go, kissed my cheek and gently pulled the white veil over my face, and he proudly walked me down the aisle, arm and arm.

CHAPTER 6

The Suffering

I believe I learned resilience from Daddy. He was amazing at picking himself up after being knocked down by life and starting over every time. I witnessed him handling disappointments, bank mergers, job changes, and business attempts that didn't last. He always brushed himself off and came up with a new plan. Sure, he'd feel bad, disappointed and a little blue for a bit, just like the rest of us. However, he never brooded or sulked for very long. His goal was always the same–to do everything in his power to provide for his family constantly.

Like the time he resigned from his role as vice president in Tuckerton, when not everyone on the board believed in his integrity or believed he was a man of his honor. He couldn't take it. His pure heart couldn't bear the thought of working for people that doubted his character. And yet, even then, he brushed himself off, found a new job and started over.

Or the many times the bank he worked for went through a merger.

Or when a friend he had placed all his trust in betrayed him.

Or even the time he closed the arcade to move back home.

And ultimately, how he valiantly fought his battle with cancer.

I recall his suffering after he received the diagnosis of cancer. The mental and emotional toll was nearly as bad as the physical destruction that wreaked havoc throughout his body. Every single one of us experienced fear and tremendous worry. It consumed us all. The relentless pain he had to endure. I prayed every day and night for our Lord to rid his body of the cancer.

It wasn't long before it spread from his prostate to his bones. It was quickly destroying him.

He had always been a handsome, fashionable man. He took great pride in his appearance. Thin build, eating Tastykake Krimpets and potato chips as he watched Monday Night Football, never gaining a pound. His attractive appearance was one thing that made him who he was.

Not that he was self-centered. The opposite, and he was never arrogant. But noticing in the mirror his good looks fading fast was a powerful hit to his self-esteem.

It finally happened. Daddy dreaded this side effect almost as much as the nausea after treatments. He lost all of his hair. My dear friend Carol's dad, John, was a barber. He graciously offered to help Daddy with a wig to boost his confidence. John showed kindness by coming to our home to prevent further upset to Daddy, and to spare Daddy from feeling embarrassed around other people in the barbershop. John fit it properly and then cut it similar to how Daddy always styled his hair.

Daddy was so appreciative and reached for his wallet. John wouldn't accept it. He put his hand out, waving at the wallet. "When you're feeling better, you can buy me a drink."

Debilitating pain constantly plagued his frail body day after day. He lost weight quickly from that point forward. Sick with nausea from the radiation treatments and narcotics for the pain, he barely ate anymore. I watched as my mother, Dawn, and my grandparents grew more and more concerned.

We are vigilant Christians that absolutely believe in the power of prayer and God's miraculous healing. It was that faith that kept me in denial and bargaining with God to bless Daddy with His life-saving hands.

Although scared and worried, I felt strong in my belief that God would heal my daddy. Confident He would answer my prayers because He knew I couldn't live without him. I continued to pray every time I thought of him, which was near constant.

He is such a great man, Lord. A terrific husband, father, brother and friend. Surely, You would want a Godly, loving man to stay on this Earth and continue to provide love and support to his family and friends. He's such an amazing witness to Your teachings, dear God. Please leave him on this Earth to continue to spread Your word. Heal him, God. Take away all his pain and suffering, but don't take him from me. I need him so.

I thought it would be over soon. His suffering. Not because I ever allowed myself to think he would die, but because I believed that the doctors themselves would be shocked to deliver the good news any day now. On every trip to the hospital for another scan and round of radiation, I believed that, on *this next visit*, the doctors would be amazed and report to my parents that the blood count had normalized. They wouldn't be able to explain it medically, of course. The fact that all of the cancer somehow vanished would be inexplicable to the medical community. Our family would give our rightful praise to God, and Daddy would happily spread the news that his Lord and savior healed his cancer!

If only…

Watching him suffer day in and day out was beyond horrible for all of us. It was heart-wrenching, to say the least.

He went for radiation treatments every few weeks that they administered through the port in his chest. It completely exhausted him each day. By the third day, he would get a burst of energy, and I allowed myself to believe it was working. He was getting better. He was going to be okay after all. There were days he was up and about and even smiling again, somewhat.

I only lived about a mile and a half away, so I would go to spend time with Daddy as much as possible to help him and Mommy whenever I could. Many times, I'd go late at night. Every time, it went something like this.

It was ten in the evening, and I was getting ready for bed. I had to get up early to get ready and drive into the next town to teach fifth grade. The house phone rang, which was odd for that time of night, so I answered quickly and with great concern. It was Daddy.

"Hi, Pooh. It's Daddy," as if I could ever mistake the sound of his voice. "Are you still up? I could use your help."

"Sure. No problem. I'll be right there. Love you."

"Thanks, Pooh. I knew I could count on you. I love you, too."

It had become somewhat of a routine for *his girls*. He was in immeasurable pain as the cancer coursed throughout the frail bones of his body. Even in agony, he was thoughtful and considerate not to ask the same daughter every night. So, we took turns.

I'd walk in the door, wearing my pajamas, faking a big smile. Mommy hid just beyond the threshold of the kitchen and living room, so Daddy wouldn't see the tears streaming down her face. Daddy lay on the living room carpet, flat on his stomach, assuming the usual position.

Falling asleep was always a challenge for him because of the persistent pain he felt all over his body.

"I'm here, Daddy."

I gave him a big kiss on his cheek and got to work. The pressure of squeezing his arms and legs would temporarily give him some relief from his suffering. I knelt next to him on the floor and prayed silently while fighting back my own tears. After the minutes turned into an hour or more, he'd feel like he might be able to sleep.

"Okay, Pooh. Can you help me go to bed now? I think it's enough. It's late. You have school tomorrow. Thank you."

I don't know how long I was on the floor squeezing his skinny arms, massaging his back and then squeezing his legs, but I would've done it forever if it would've taken his excruciating pain away.

The following Sunday at mass stands out clearly in my mind.

Sacred Heart Church was both a stunning cathedral in its own right and a sentimental place our family attended every week since I can remember. Four sections of pews spanned across the church from left to right, with a massive center aisle pointing towards the altar. Fourteen giant, stained glass arched windows allowed just the right amount of sunlight to enter God's house. Each portrayed beautiful visions of the Stations of the Cross. Huge marble pillars divided the outer aisles from the center. The white marble wall at the back of the altar came to a rounded ceiling and donned several smaller stained glass windows at the top. A giant and intricately carved wooden crucifix in the middle just behind the altar table. As I walked halfway down the center aisle, I lowered my knee and blessed myself as I entered our usual pew with my family.

I focused my gaze on the beautiful crucifix and I stared desperately at Jesus Christ as I prayed. I thought about how our Lord suffered on the cross and about how Daddy is now suffering from his own torturous pain every day.

The stunning balcony behind me echoed the emotional sounds of the organ. As the cantor sang "On Eagles Wings", I struggled to fight back my tears.

It became increasingly difficult for my father to sit, kneel, stand and kneel again as much as is required during Catholic mass. I secretly watched him, out of the corner of my eye, as he moved slowly and with the squint of anguish, his wrinkled forehead and jaw clenching. Despite his great pain, he knelt before God, praying for the same answer we all prayed for.

Again, I prayed for my daddy.

God, look at Your faithful son praising You despite his great pain. Heal his illness, dear Lord. Take his pain away, but PLEASE don't take him from me.

A moment later, Daddy struggled to stand for the 'Our Father'. I don't know how he summoned the strength, but that poor man raised his arms above his shoulders, outstretched to the heavens, as we all prayed aloud together.

Daddy struggled to make it through a typical workday at Sun National Bank. Before, he hardly ever called out sick, but everything changed after his cancer diagnosis. Work had just become too much for him. He couldn't think as clearly, distracted by the pain, and had difficulties driving his car while extremely nauseous.

By May 1999, Daddy no longer drove his own car. It wasn't often that he ventured out of the house by then, except for Sunday mass. It got so bad he rarely wanted to go anywhere.

My grandfather, Frank Panzino, passed away after an extended illness. He lived in Lehighton,

Pennsylvania, and Daddy didn't think he could handle the long drive. We all knew deep down he had to say his goodbyes to his father. Mommy's parents, my Nonni and Poppop, insisted on driving him over two hours to the funeral.

It was July 1999. Daddy struggled to kneel in front of his father's casket. The worry for Daddy overshadowed my sadness over losing my grandfather. The long drive had really put him over the edge. He looked weaker than usual, and the pain on his haggard face was heart-wrenching. Standing nearby in case he needed my help to stand, I heard Daddy praying. Then I froze where I stood, saddened by I heard him say.

"I love you, Dad. I'll see you soon."

Shock ran through me. My debilitating denial could not allow that phrase to make sense in my mind.

Why would he say that? What does that mean? I know he's suffering, but he will not be next! Why would he think that?

There have been many times since my father's passing that I, too, have had to endure suffering. I think of him often, but especially during the difficult times in my life as I struggle to pull myself together.

Life is a rollercoaster with extreme highs and terrifying falls. The challenge lies in learning to expect the unexpected and cope with heartbreaks in a healthy way.

As a full-time teacher, single mom of two and dealing with the issues of raising a child with Down syndrome, I often feel as though I'm burning the candle at both ends. I grow weary that my daddy is not here to encourage me and light the path I face ahead.

It gets more difficult to start over after each shock. There have been many times I felt as though I reached my limit. Hurt, betrayed and disappointed multiple times in my life. I often doubted myself. I used to wonder if I could actually summon the strength to go on once again.

There were often many times that I wanted to curl up in a ball to cry after a divorce or scream into a pillow, struggling to raise a child with special needs. Other times I drive to the Padre Pio shrine daily to beg for help.

I would then remember how Daddy led my example, forging ahead in life after every setback.

My intention was to guide my son into adulthood by showing courage and self-confidence, hoping that he would do the same in his own life. I have to dig deep and remember who I am. I need to set an example of faith and determination. Through my strength of will, I could find a way to press on. I learned to not second guess myself. I rely on the anchors in my past, times I picked myself up after falling, to find the strength to keep going once again and continue to fight for the life I truly want.

In those dark times, I remember the lessons I've learned from my father.

Honesty and integrity build character and earn the respect of others.

Self-respect creates confidence and happiness.

Kindness to all people was non-negotiable as a true child of God.

I'm reminded that quitting when faced with challenges in life is not an option.

Daddy never sat me down for a speech or a life lesson conversation, per se. He led by example, and I watched him closely. So now, in times of trouble, because of him, in honor of his fight, I have the necessary tools to move on.

I put my own broken pieces back together.

I brush myself off and stand tall.

I hold my head high because I know who I came from.

And so, I begin again.

CHAPTER 7

Salvatore

Salvatore Panzino was born to Josephine and Frank on December 30, 1942. He was the youngest of three. The oldest, Frank Jr., and the middle child, Mary. They all lived together and endured frequent arguments between their parents. The children witnessed a tumultuous marriage that ended in divorce. Their young family was torn apart when he was only three years old.

Frank Jr. and Mary ended up in an orphanage. Unable to physically handle or financially afford all three children, his grandmother, Francis Panzino, only took little Sammy to live with her.

Family and friends always called him Sammy. He learned from a very young age about their Catholic and Italian values and traditions.

Every Sunday, she dressed him up and combed his hair as if he was heading to a modeling photo shoot. He sat beside her, well-behaved, at mass week after week. After church, she placed authentic, home-cooked Italian pasta dishes on the small kitchen table with love.

As time passed, Frank and Mary came home to live with Sammy and their grandmother. Now that their mother, Josephine, recovered from the divorce, she desperately wanted to be together with all of her children. They lived in a small home in which the boys shared a bedroom.

There were several acres between their home and their cousin's home next door, which provided many opportunities for the kids to run back and forth to play and spend time together. Josephine was close with her Rambone side of the family, so it was natural that the cousins grew up enjoying one another for many years. It was not only convenient, but enjoyable for the kids and the adults to spend quality, family time with one another. During his younger years, Sammy, Frank and Mary enjoyed laughter and fun times on their grandmother's Newfield farm. They had plenty of land in which to run and play and help with the chores. Their grandmother had beautiful, dark brown and white horses that roamed the property. Sammy loved the freedom and joy of riding the horses every chance he got.

His older brother, Frank, had served in the Navy, so it seemed natural for Sammy to consider the military when he came of age. He enlisted in the Army right after graduating from Vineland High School in 1961.

After returning home having served in the Army, most of which in Korea, he continued close friendships with several young men from all over the country. They became lifelong friends after enduring those difficult four years together. His time in the service served him well as his loyalty, honor and sense of responsibility was ingrained deeper into his being.

He had a broad smile when surrounded by his friends and family. He was five foot ten with a slender build and, even though it was mid-December, always had an olive, tan complexion. A handsome, Italian man with a full head of dark hair, a thin face and a chiseled jawline. He dressed fashionably for the time, complete with rings, gold bracelets and a miraculous gold medal of the Blessed Mother.

Coming from a broken home, he wanted nothing more than to love and honor his wife and provide all he could for her and *his girls*. He was loyal, devoted and the life of every party or family gathering.

He had a slight bounce to his step, especially as he socialized from room to room at a family event. Quite the prankster, he often teased and joked with everyone in a fun, loving way.

Fast Forward to the 1980s, Z. Cavariccis, Jordache jeans, gold chains and bracelets, Hugo Boss sweatshirts and football jerseys were the majority of Daddy's hip style outside of the usual office suits during the week. He took pride in his appearance from his Ray-Bans and perfectly combed hair down to his matching shoes.

He was the type of man who never demanded respect. He didn't have to. Everyone who knew him had deep respect and admiration for him. His constant displays of love and support created trust and appreciation, especially from *his girls*. He could always rise up and start anew every time he got knocked down in life.

Daddy was a diligent worker and a devoted family man who never missed Catholic mass on Sunday. He maintained a respectful attitude towards his parents and in-laws, regardless of their words or involvement in our lives. He possessed qualities of kindness and loyalty and knew how to find joy in life. He enjoyed bustin' chops and bringing laughter to others. Everyone who knew him loved him dearly.

He was one of the good guys.

Army pic 1960

Me and Daddy on the Carousel

Daddy

Dawny and Daddy 1984

The Look

Daddy and Me my birthday

Daddy and Mommy Poconos 1983

My HS grad party 1990

Me and Daddy at family wedding 1991

Best friends

Fighting over Daddy 1992

Christmas 1992

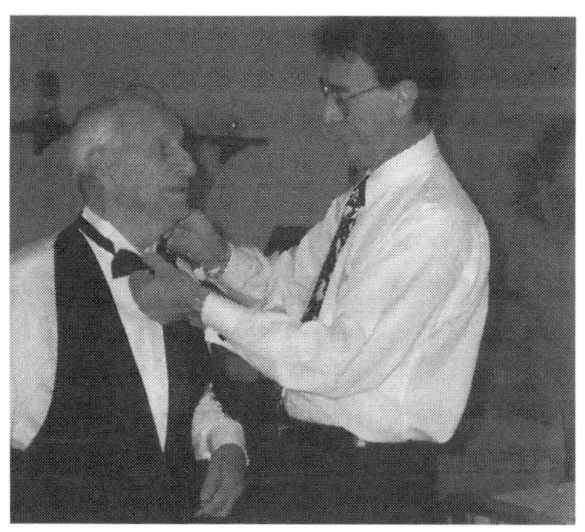

Daddy and Poppop 1996

Daddy Daughter Dance 1996

Me and Daddy Family Wedding

CHAPTER 8

Soulmates

Theirs was a love–beautiful and true.

It all began in Vineland, NJ. Landis Avenue was the hotspot for friends and couples to meet and hang out in the 60s.

Barbara drove down 'The Ave' in her new, white convertible with the top down. Her jet black hair brushed perfectly and firmly sprayed with Aqua Net, and a slight curl just above her shoulders. She wore lipstick, the perfect shade of pink, to accentuate her beautiful smile. Singing along with The Beatles to 'I Wanna Hold Your Hand' and Tom Jones' 'It's Not Unusual' as she drove slowly to see where her friends were hanging out. Then it started to rain.

She quickly pulled over and put it in park. She had closed the roof on her own before but this time struggled to secure the ragtop. The drizzle was quickly turning to a steady rain. Barbara wasn't sure which worried her more, the car interior getting wet or her hair.

Just then, a handsome man pulled up beside her in his friend's car.

"Can I help you with that?"

"Oh yes, thank you."

"I'm Sammy."

"Hi. I'm Barbara," she blushed as he flashed a flirtatious smile.

Once the roof was secure, and her hair was safe under a storefront awning, they stood together talking and laughing for quite some time.

Sammy was polite and respectful. He confidently kept his eyes fixed on hers. Barbara was soft-spoken but giggled and smiled as they talked about family, finishing school and the Army.

She thanked him again for his help and explained she had a curfew. Sammy walked her to the car and opened the door for her. He leaned on the door flashing one more smile before saying goodnight.

Minutes later, when Barbara arrived home, her mother asked her how her night was. She always waited up for her only child before she turned in for the evening. Barbara excitedly told her mother all about the handsome boy she met on 'The Ave' and how he helped her.

"Mom, tonight I met the man I'm going to marry."

A week later, Barbara Spinelli waited in the back of Sacred Heart church. She stood proudly, as a confirmation sponsor, beside her young cousin. A rule-follower and Italian-Catholic girl, beautiful inside and out, she knew the proper way to behave in church more than anyone.

Suddenly she heard…

psst… psst…

She wouldn't dare turn her head. The role of confirmation sponsor was not to be taken lightly, so she maintained her focus down the long aisle as she waited her turn to escort her candidate.

There it was again. This time she heard her name.

"Psst… psst… Barb…"

She couldn't believe it. She had been dreaming about him all week, praying she would see him again. The broad, handsome smile was once again taking her breath away.

"Sammy?" less worried now about breaking the rule of talking during mass, she smiled back, not realizing he had already filed in beside her. "What are you doing here?"

"I'm a sponsor too," he said, pointing to the young boy next to him.

"Ssshhh," she smiled and tried to regain her focus. "Let's talk after the ceremony."

After the service, they talked outside of the church and planned their first official date.

Days later, Barbara sat in a steakhouse in Atlantic City unable to stop smiling. She knew fancy clothes and expensive things were never part of his childhood. She also knew that Sammy grew up in a family with strong values of honesty, family first and faith in God. He talked and talked, and Barbara smiled, thinking he was the ideal catch. Sammy told her about his early years and broken home and explained that he believed marriage should be, and for him, would be, forever. He told Barbara, who was already smitten, he planned to work hard and do whatever he needed to do in order to give his family everything he never had.

Wrapped up in conversation and enjoying each other's company, Sammy was almost late bringing her home that night. Arriving at the Spinelli residence on time, they continued talking in the driveway and laughing. Saying their goodbyes on the porch after he walked her to the door, the outside lights began to flicker off and on again. Recognizing the signal, they stepped into the foyer. Just as they were about to kiss goodnight, the hall light turned on. Not realizing what was happening, Sammy turned the light off to kiss Barbara goodnight once more. The light just above their heads quickly turned on again. Interrupted once more, Sammy looked up and, from the corner of his eye, saw Mr. Spinelli at the top of the stairs with his hand on the light switch. Before Sammy had the chance to greet him, he bellowed from the top of the stairs.

"You're late!"

Barbara spoke, although respectfully, in defense of Sammy in an effort to keep him out of trouble.

"Daddy, we were here on time. We have been talking in the driveway."

"If you weren't in this door, then you're late," he replied sternly, although with a half smile.

Sammy apologized and tried to take the blame which only made her father smile more.

As Barbara said goodbye, she started up the stairs towards her old-fashioned father. She looked back over her shoulder to smile at Sammy and thank him for a lovely evening.

"Okay, the night's over. You can go."

"Goodnight, Mr. Spinelli. See you soon."

"Yeah, yeah. Goodbye, Sammy. And, oh yeah, drive safe."

Her mother stood just beyond the door waiting for the juicy 'boy talk'. She rushed over to her mother and said again that he was the one.

When asked how she knew, Barbara replied, "He smiled, and when he did, I knew."

Barbara Spinelli and Salvatore Panzino were married less than a year later, May 28, 1966, at the ages of twenty and twenty-three.

They started their young family with the birth of Dawn in March 1967. The youngest was born in January five years later.

Their love, commitment and happiness was infectious. They raised their daughters with constant affection, tenderness and encouragement. Life wasn't perfect. There were health problems, family issues and financial struggles. But, as true soulmates do, they faced their difficulties head-on, knowing they could get through life's obstacles together.

Dawn and I grew up happy to witness their special connection. Their love not only taught us what a marriage should be, but it gave us a sense of security.

There are countless examples of their love for one another that flood my fondest memories. One of my favorite instances was at a family wedding.

The crowded ballroom echoed with music so deafening I had to shout just to be heard by the person sitting right next to me. Happy to be a guest at my first family wedding, I was on the dance floor more often than sitting at my table.

As a pre-teen, the excitement and delight of being all dressed up and twirling on the dance floor was absolutely thrilling. I wore a new dress with a black satin bottom that waved in the air as I turned. The top of the dress was checkered black and white and met at the waist with a big satin bow tied in the back. Black tights and brand new black, patent leather shoes completed my ensemble. I was having the time of my life. As I recall, they were my first pair of heels other than my weekly tap shoes. They were only an inch or two high, but I felt so grown up and loved the way they clickety-clacked across the dance floor. Almost as satisfying as my tap shoes.

Surrounded by family that night in particular, I felt confident that nothing could be better than dancing to music at an enormous party with family and friends.

Then, as I was dancing across the floor from person to person and twirling around my sister and cousins, I stopped dead in my tracks.

I noticed Daddy sitting at a nearby table, looking out onto the dance floor with a huge smile on his face. Daddy smiled and laughed almost all the time, especially when surrounded by his family, but this wasn't just any smile, though. Rather, an expression of pure love and pride. I wasn't sure why at first, so I followed his line of sight across the crowded dance floor all the way to my mother. She was laughing and dancing with a group of people, having a wonderful time. He was just happily watching her, thoroughly enjoying the moment. I remember realizing, with hundreds of people in the ballroom, all he cared about, in that moment, was his beautiful wife. She was completely unaware of his admiration at the time. She was just purely being herself, always beautiful, always sweet and kind, friendly and caring to everyone. He clearly admired her and was simply enjoying watching her have a great time.

It was right then and there I remember thinking to myself, *Dear God, I hope one day a wonderful man looks at me the way my father looks at my mother.*

As I grew older, I noticed their interactions more and more.

They were the epitome of a wonderful marriage and set the perfect example of mutual love and respect in a relationship. Everyone always admired Barb and Sammy. They put so much thoughtfulness and care into each day. Saying hello and goodbye, they gave each other three kisses every day. The way they held pinkies walking anywhere together. The instant smile that appeared when they caught the others' eye.

Mommy made his favorite home-cooked meals and was sure to have it on the table only minutes after he returned home from work. She even made the nauseating liver and onions dish with care. No one liked it except for Daddy, but that didn't stop her from cooking it special just for him. She cooked for him with love, and he always was appreciative. So on those nights, she'd make a separate dinner for everyone else.

He was a less-than-healthy eater.

Reaching for a second slice of Italian bread and slathering it with butter and sugar was a common occurrence. He'd add three teaspoons of sugar to his coffee and say, "Pass the cow."

He always prayed and gave thanks to God and his beautiful wife before every meal.

Mommy was the traditional wonderful wife. She, of course, completed all the typical housekeeping chores. She proudly waited on him every chance she could. A plate of cookies with a Yoo-hoo or chips with a root beer while watching the Cowboys. I noticed she took great pride, in particular, in ironing his suit shirts. It was more personal because it was just for him.

Daddy was grateful for everything she did for him. He would thank her and compliment her often. He loved doing all he could for his wife.

He was both thoughtful and romantic.

Without fail, he would buy a brand new 45 record every Christmas. Each year, he chose a different love song that captured their essence as a couple or showcased his immense love for her. She would squeal with delight each year, expecting the tradition but excited to see which song it would be this Christmas.

Air Supply would blare through the living room the minute she opened it… *I'm so lost without you….* They would hug and kiss, and before you knew it, they were slow-dancing in front of their adoring daughters watching from in front of our Christmas tree.

There were many times, some when she'd least expect it and some for no particular reason, he would come home with a fresh bouquet of her favorite flowers or a new piece of gold jewelry. She, of course, made a big deal and was very appreciative.

All of those little things are actually the big things in a relationship. The building blocks of love and respect that continue to grow and nurture a strong, happy marriage.

They had *it.*

They knew.

Everyone else witnessed it.

It came so naturally to both of them. Even as the weeks turned into months which rolled into years that just flew by raising their girls and working hard. Me and my sister were truly blessed to experience their love for each other as well as the love they freely gave to both of us.

CHAPTER 9

The Unthinkable

It was a Saturday morning. August 14, 1999.

I was putting a long skirt on and a frilly blouse, excited to meet my sister-in-law, Kim, for a Mary Kay breakfast event.

The phone rang.

"G, get here quick. It's not good."

I was in the car and on the road in less than a minute. I wasn't crying. I *still* wasn't even worried. The only way I can describe it was as if time stood still. I don't remember the drive there, or even parking, or going up the hospital elevator. I do, however, remember walking into his hospital room.

That moment was a vision I hate to recall, and I know I will never forget.

As I'm typing this very moment, twenty-two years later, I hate to put it in print. Part of me feels like it's too personal. It was a private, personal moment. My Daddy in his last moments. He's mine, and you don't get to know him the way I did.

Then, I remember why I am writing this book. I know that many of you reading this right now have suffered a great loss. My intention, despite the circumstances that stole your loved one from your life, is for you to know you are not alone in grief. I would like to think that sharing my pain eases yours, even just a little. The purpose of sharing my Daddy with you is not only to honor what an amazing man he was but to help you cope with your own great loss. In hearing my experience, we are connected by our sorrow. So that something devastating and sad may help us to feel like someone else understands. And maybe we won't feel so alone.

So… the instant I walked into his hospital room, I was pushed out, although I kept my eyes on him. I don't remember who was there. Of course Mommy and my sister, Dawn, but I saw no one but him. I couldn't tell you if there were doctors, nurses, men, women or how many were in the room. My focus was on Daddy, and although they held me back, my eyes were fixed on him.

I wish they weren't.

It was heart-wrenching and a terrible sight to see, but I couldn't take my eyes off of my Daddy.

The paddles were out. Someone yelled "clear" and shoved me out of the way. His skinny, frail body flew up off the bed and flopped back down.

They got him back.

I found out later they put him through that horrible ordeal once before, waiting for us to get there, so he had the chance to say goodbye to *his girls*.

I rushed over to him. I held his hand, squeezed it tight, and I felt him grasp onto my hand. I said, "Daddy, it's me. Gina. I'm here. It's okay. I'm here."

His eyes opened for just an instant and closed slowly. He squeezed my hand. He squeezed Mommy and Dawn as he held onto them with his other hand.

And with that, he was gone.

Nothing mattered anymore.

After his passing, I was numb. Numb and angry. We were so close. We had such a special bond. Not only did I have the utmost respect for him as my father, but I felt as though he was my best friend. He was an incredible listener and gave the most loving, honest advice. He was so good at loving us… me. I was his little girl, his Pooh bear, and I completely idolized him. The devastation was unbearable. I was twenty-seven years old, and he was only fifty-six when he passed.

As sick as he had been the last couple of years, I had convinced myself that this day wouldn't come for decades later. He was so good. A wonderful father, husband and friend. I still found myself asking God why. The anger was almost all-consuming.

Why him, dear God? And with my sister having his first grandchild in a couple of months, why now, God!?

I was pissed. I doubted my faith. I questioned everything now. I was so sure that a dear, benevolent, all-knowing God would answer my prayers. Afterall, He knew how special Daddy was. He knew how we all adored him. How could He take him away from us!?

Much of what happened those first several days after his death is still a blur. I remember bits and pieces of visitors and planning the funeral.

I felt as though I was an apathetic blob in space and time. Everyone was moving at warp speed around me, but I had no idea what anyone was doing or what they were saying. I was in absolute denial, which would surprise some of you knowing I had watched him suffer and wither away as he battled cancer for two years.

Constant, endless people poured in at my parents' house, and hoards of food covered the kitchen counters and table. I know dozens of people hugged me, but I can only remember a handful of faces. Not because they weren't all important people in my life. They were. I was just dazed and confused. The more they talked about him, the more I ate. I remember thinking,

They can't be talking about my Daddy. He was supposed to be healed. God wouldn't do this to me. This can't be real.

My mind knew he was gone, but my heart wouldn't fully accept it. I was in shock that God actually allowed this to happen. I was in a fog, dazed and confused, just going through the motions of my life. I don't recall many conversations, people, waking up or getting dressed.

Dawn and I stayed with Mommy for several days. Neither of us could bear the thought of her being alone there without her soulmate. At night, we slept with our mother, one of us on either side of her. We held her night after night and all sobbed together, not saying a word until we finally fell asleep from exhaustion.

The next morning, I sat with Mommy and Dawn to choose the best church hymns and which readings from the bible should be read at the funeral mass. Who will sing? Who will read? Which flowers?

I ate two donuts, and that was after a bagel and cream cheese.

I thought about Daddy raising his feeble arms to God, singing aloud to "On Eagles Wings". I knew it was the best choice but wouldn't allow myself to read the lyrics in the booklet in front of us, knowing it would rip my heart out.

All white flowers. White lillies, peace lilies, white carnations and white roses. They were his favorites. He deserved the best. We must choose what he would have wanted.

Many aunts, uncles and close friends were in and out for days. Someone actually had the audacity to say, "he's in a better place." That pissed me off. I walked away. Oh, I know she meant well, and her intentions were good. What can people really say? I'm sure I've said awful things with good intentions at a funeral. Luckily, if they're anything like me, they won't remember my lame attempts at consoling their grief.

I just didn't respond and thought,

How can any place be better than with us? He's supposed to be with me!

I then gorged on several chocolate chip cookies.

I was twenty-seven, newly married and an absolute daddy's girl. My life was, in many ways, just beginning, and he was supposed to be here for it. I didn't have children but knew I would in a couple years. They needed a Poppop. This was so unfair. I was so confused by it all. The more my mind raced with the notions of Daddy actually not being here on Earth with us, the more I ate.

He was gone.

I am very aware and grateful to be blessed with so many family and friends that were there for us in our time of need. But I was in such a state of shock and still somehow unable to fully grasp the fact that Daddy would no longer be in my life. I just sat in a stupor on the living room sofa thinking about all that he would miss… all I would miss… how this cannot be real… wondering how I would go on.

I'd force myself to stop thinking, and I'd do whatever I could to be numb and stop feeling. I mindlessly consumed every casserole, lasagna, stuffed shell, pie, donut and cookie that was brought into the house.

My mind wandered off to thousands of special occasions, events and holidays over the years. Thoughts raced, and it was near impossible to stop imagining the terrible life without him.

I thought about the day I'd have children and envisioned what an amazing poppop he would've been. I grew more angry.

He had so much love to give. I would never have the privilege of watching his face beam with pure joy holding his grandchildren.

I was pissed off! How could God rob him of that privilege?

He wouldn't get to love them the way he loved me.

I ate even more.

The thought that my children would never know how amazing, loving and fun their grandfather was absolutely crushed me.

It was beyond devastating.

For the first time in my life, I actually felt my heart break.

My poor sister, Dawn, was seven months pregnant with his first grandchild. She had hoped and prayed that he would hold on to see her. Samantha Lynn was the first of four grandchildren over the next six years that he would miss out on. We would call her Sammi after Daddy, of course. My father's name was Salvatore. Many people, mostly our family and close friends, called him Sammy.

The funeral was the next day. We picked Daddy's favorite brown suit he used to wear to the bank.

He always enjoyed wearing a suit and tie.

We helped Mommy decide what she would wear. She cried at every option until she remembered something Daddy said.

"He always loved me in this one."

Dawn and I wrapped her in a hug and cried.

I then realized that after more than a week of eating my feelings, my black dresses were now too tight.

I will never forget going out in public for the first time since *the unthinkable*. I had no choice but to go buy a new black dress for my father's funeral. One of my best friends, Shelly, drove me to the mall and was so supportive and loving. She parked at the entrance where she knew a clothing store would be right near the doors.

It was crowded in the mall. I didn't want to be seen by anyone. It didn't feel 'right'. The world was still turning. People bustling from here to there, talking and even laughing. It was as if I was outside of my body watching the activity. I felt angry.

Why were all the people going about their daily lives?

Didn't they realize what just happened?

How can the world be turning and all these people moving on without him?!

I couldn't fathom going on without my Daddy. It was a strange, horrible feeling being out in public. I was empty inside. I went numb again and forced myself not to think. I rushed into the first clothing store, with Shelly, and grabbed the first black dress I found. I couldn't wait to get out of there.

Oh, how I miss his smile.

The dreadful day arrived. The black limousine pulled into the driveway to pick us up for the service. Someone announced, “It’s time to go.”

There we stood at the front door, *his girls,* dressed in black. Shaking and holding onto one another, we walked out of the door stepping out into a terrible new world without him.

CHAPTER 10

The First of Many

Walking my fifth graders down the hallway, I was in a daze.

I don't belong here. I don't want to go on without him. Why am I here?

It was only two weeks after my father's passing. It felt too soon.

I hated that the world was still turning. Everyone going about their lives as if nothing happened felt… wrong. And here I am stumbling through life, lost and confused, not knowing how to live without him. Didn't they know that the world had just lost one of the good guys?

I was angry. Angry that God had taken him from me. And yet felt guilty for such blasphemy. Afterall, my father had raised a good, Catholic girl. How could I be mad at God? I felt disoriented, and most days I walked around and hated the world – everything and everyone. What's worse was that I knew I couldn't do anything about it. There was an immense void inside of me now. Filled with incredible pain and deep sadness. I didn't want to live without him, but I knew I could never take my own life, even if I wanted to, for fear I would disappoint him. I was, after all, his Pooh bear. He always wanted what was best for me. He'd want me to not just live my life but to thrive and find happiness.

So I had to stay here on Earth without him. Forced to shuffle aimlessly through this life without his love, without his wisdom, without his support, without hearing the roar of his laughter.

I was deeply saddened and falling into a depression.

I was a fifth grade teacher at the time, only twenty-seven years old. I absolutely hated the fact that I had to go on in life without him. And there I was, in a fog, feeling numb, walking my fifth graders down the hallway to the gym.

Just then, one of my students stepped out of line. Agitated and filled with grief, I senselessly barked at him and scolded him for stepping out of line. He continued and bent down to the floor. As I watched to see what he was doing, I realized he picked something up. He brought it straight to me with a smile on his face and put it in my hand.

He looked me right in the eye and said, "This is for you."

My heart skipped a beat. I looked into my hand. It took my breath away, and I stood frozen in the hallway. I got a chill, and goosebumps covered my arms.

I hadn't seen, or even thought of one, in over twenty years. Tears filled my eyes, fixed on…

A red quarter.

Overwhelmed with a wave of emotion, I smiled for the first time in weeks. And in that moment, I felt my father's presence.

The little boy had been standing there, watching quietly with the rest of my class. They recognized my amazement and then finally asked, "What is it?"

I didn't respond right away. I thought about how the little boy had never even looked at what he grabbed from the floor, and yet somehow, he instinctively knew it was mine.

I looked up at my students after what seemed like several minutes and replied, "It's a gift from Heaven."

There is no living soul that could ever convince me that that specific red quarter, the first of many, was not actually heaven-sent. A gift from my Daddy.

He knows how I struggle to accept the fact that he is gone. He knows I have to learn, somehow, to go on in this life without him. He knows I needed confirmation that he was still, and always would be, with me, by my side in life. He knows it has to be something rare, something special only to us, for me to believe, beyond a shadow of doubt, that it was from him.

My mind flashed back to memories from many years ago in our very own arcade. I was skipping around with my sister, playing Pac-Man after school. The speakers in Obsession played "Jack and Diane", and laughter of children filled the air as Daddy watched with that great big smile of his. He handed us another roll of red quarters to put in the machines to play.

For the first time during the last two weeks since he passed, I had a glimmer of hope for my new life. Peace filled my heart knowing not only was he okay, he was also no longer suffering. Without even closing my eyes, I could see his broad smile and the love in his eyes. I felt overwhelmed with his ever present love. I knew, inside the depths of my soul, it was a message from my Daddy. He was still there reassuring me as he always had, letting me know he was still with me and that everything would be okay. I thought maybe if he was okay that somehow, eventually, I would be okay too. I knew he would want me to be more than okay and that I must go on.

That was the first of many red quarters. The beginning of countless signs, messages and little hellos from Daddy each of us received throughout different times in our lives since his passing.

When distress in life was too hard to handle.

When wonderful celebrations occurred, and we missed him dearly.

When we'd least expected it but needed him the most.

Then, always at just the right moment, even better than *pennies from heaven*, we would receive red quarters…

CHAPTER 11

More Red Quarters from Heaven

1994

Daddy had such a positive impact on everyone he came across but especially friends of mine and my sisters.

As we became young adults in our early twenties, it was even more common for him to become friends with our friends. Dawn had an amazing group of friends that she would go out with that would come to the house and get to know Daddy pretty well. In my personal experience, most Italians love to play cards. So as soon as her friends talked about poker night and invited him along, he was more than happy to agree.

He would go to the guy's townhouse in Hammonton every week. They, of course, were required to have a box of Snyder's hard pretzels just for him. It had to be the ones in the box. Whoever was lucky enough to sit next to him during the game and made a wisecrack about the Dallas Cowboys, or just busting chops as a group of guys playing poker will do, he'd give that crooked sideways look, and then *boom*, you got punched in the arm. You also got a punch in the arm if he had a better hand than you as he left and teased you about it. Many nights, those poor guys would leave with a sore arm.

However, every one of them would happily take another bruise to have one more night enjoying Mr. Panzino.

His laugh was infectious, and he was a pure joy to be around. They all miss him so very much.

What's ironic and mind-blowing to me is that while preparing for this book by talking to people about Daddy, Matt, a friend of Dawn's, informed me that sometimes Daddy would find a red quarter in the pot during those poker games. Without sharing his memory of the arcade and how he painted them for *his girls*, he would just quietly take out the red quarters and replace them with different quarters. Then he'd carefully place it in his pocket to save for himself.

Knowing Daddy the way I do, I'm sure during those poker nights, he remembered *his girls* playing in Obsession decades prior, and smiled.

We never knew until now.

2000

Daddy was always so proud of Mommy and encouraged her to work towards her goals. It was because of his support that she was able to take more classes and complete the certifications necessary to succeed. She was the recycling coordinator for the county and, later, the city of Vineland. He beamed whenever he spoke of her to others.

Mommy was struggling to return to work after losing her soulmate. Only a few short months after Daddy passed, she had a public speaking event out of town. She especially loved the speaking engagements for children. She believed that educating them on the importance of recycling would be her small part to improve their futures. She spoke to several classes in elementary schools that day about the differences of recycled items and what should or shouldn't be recycled. She thought of how proud her husband would've been on that day in particular.

It was pouring rain by the time the event finished, and everyone made a mad dash for their buses and cars. Children and adults alike ran through the parking lot to get out of the rain.

Mommy, in her stylish business dress suit, hurried with her matching umbrella as best as she could in her heels. She heard a little boy from one of the classes call out to her, and although she was getting wet, she stopped suddenly. He yelled over the noise of the rain.

"You dropped this! Here."

"No, honey. I don't think it's mine."

"Ma'am, it is yours. This is for you."

He reached out his little hand and placed it into hers. He quickly ran off to get out of the rain and onto his school bus.

Mommy didn't want to be fully wet, so she did the same. In the driver's seat and protected from the rain, she finally looked at what the young boy handed her.

It was a red quarter.

She smiled through her tears knowing that her Sammy was with her after all. She felt the warmth of his love and pride after her first recycling presentation since he passed.

2002

I lay in the delivery room, more than ready to deliver my first born.

Ironically, it was Labor Day, and I had been in excruciating pain for several hours. I had all intentions to deliver naturally. And then, that idea was thrown out the window along with my pleasant demeanor as time went on.

I begged for an epidural as I cried in my tenth hour of pain. The doctor explained that I was too far along, and it was too late to administer an epidural at this point. They were able to give a different pain medication through an IV but only just before I gave birth.

My husband was by my side but unable to sit in either of the two chairs available. I'm sure he would have loved to get off his feet after standing at my bedside all night, but I said he couldn't.

In the delusion of the meds finally kicking in, I informed him that there were no seats available. He looked confused.

"What do you mean? There are two chairs right here."

I laughed. "You can't sit with them. Daddy and Mickey Mouse are sitting there."

Matthew Salvatore arrived healthy, screaming and crying at 7:00 p.m.

Mommy, Dawn, Nonni and Poppop were all waiting down the hall. After waiting for hours, they went to the cafeteria and the gift shop. My sister, Matthew's proud godmother, was not at all surprised to get another red quarter in her change that day.

2002

My sister, Dawn, had a very special bond and close relationship with Daddy as well. She shared her wonderful memories of Daddy bringing her to Phillies games. Pete Rose and Mike Schmidt were our favorite players. It was a big deal going to live games as a child, and it was just one of many ways he bonded with *his girls*.

One October night at Veterans Stadium, Dawn sat next to Daddy, excited for the first pitch. As she sat with her pretzel, ice cream and soda, the crowd roared. Screaming fans, light blue jerseys and burgundy Phillies hats blanketed the stands.

It was the playoff game that sent the Phillies to the World Series, 1980.

Dawn had the thrill of sharing in the explosive cheers happy to watch the Phillies win with her Daddy.

It was that memory that made bringing her daughter, Samantha, to Phillies games extra special.

Sammi, named after her grandfather, never knew Daddy. He passed two months before his first of four grandchildren were born.

It was bittersweet for Dawn to carry on the tradition taking her own daughter to Phillies games. Sammi was only three years old, but Dawn started telling stories of Poppop Sal as we all did with the next generation. Dawn thought about all the good times and told Sammi stories of watching the Phillies with her grandfather.

She mentioned several times that he would love to be there for Sammi's first game. It was the seventh inning stretch, and, of course, in addition to the other thousands of people in the stadium, everyone went to get cold drinks, food and ice cream.

Dawn and Sammi's father each got in two different lines for ice cream to double their chances of getting to the register to order as fast as possible.

After an already grueling wait with a three-year-old, Dawn thought she'd just forget it. A soft serve twist with rainbow sprinkles in the miniature, plastic baseball helmet wasn't worth this line.

Then she remembered how Daddy always endured a long line for her. Happy to wait if it meant getting one of *his girls* the special treat they wanted.

Dawn stayed in line talking to Daddy in her mind.

Not long after her decision, the line suddenly moved quickly. They finally reach the counter, and Sammi got her ice cream helmet. As she paid, she told the young man to keep the change. He declined politely, but Dawn said, "You keep it," with a smile.

The boy looked her right in the eye and kindly insisted, "This is for you."

She put her hand out for the change, and her eyes filled with tears. The young man handed her a red quarter.

The tears flowed as she smiled and knew in her heart Daddy was there after all, sharing in the fun times at the stadium with his granddaughter just as he always had with Dawn.

They didn't stop there, the special times with the kids he never got to meet. The times he, the dedicated family man, would have never missed. Yet, he still makes his presence known from Heaven.

2006

To say my second pregnancy was stressful is an understatement.

Only a few months into the pregnancy, obstetricians ordered more bloodwork and ultrasounds than usual. I was thirty-four years old and because of a scare that turned out to be nothing during my first pregnancy, the doctors labeled me 'high risk'.

I lay on the exam table for my first ultrasound. We were excited to learn if it was another boy or our first girl. My husband held my hand as he stared at the computer screen. The technician drew a box around a tiny section of my unborn child and then typed 'abnormal'. My husband squeezed my hand so tight that I looked at his face and knew something was terribly wrong.

We went to a great number of appointments over the worrisome months that followed. We soon learned that my daughter had Down syndrome.

It was a difficult pill to swallow. We were shocked and frightened. We were uneducated at the time and concerned about what that would mean for her, Matthew and our family's future. Later testing determined that in addition to her special needs diagnosis, her organs were filling with fluid and growing disproportionately. Her life was in danger. And possibly mine as well.

All I did was cry and pray for the next couple of months.

Soon after, I underwent an experimental surgery.

The doctors' hands shook visibly after what seemed to be multiple cups of coffee that morning. Yet as he inserted the ten-inch needle into my pregnant belly, he was surprisingly still.

The room was full of doctors and nurses scurrying around my gurney as many medical students stood nearby writing on their clipboards. A runner quickly grabbed Faith's extracted blood and literally ran it down the stairs to be put through a centrifuge. He quickly returned to provide the medical teams with her specific blood type and count numbers. The doctor was still sitting like a statue, not moving a millimeter. The slightest movement would prove disastrous for me, my unborn baby girl or both of us.

The in-utero, blood transfusion was an astonishing success. My girl had a couple more weeks to grow safely inside me.

That October, six weeks early, Faith was taken with an emergency c-section. By the grace of God, Faith pulled through and continued to fight. I thought of Daddy often and believed she inherited that fighting spirit from her grandfather. I talked to him often as I prayed during those stressful several months.

At five months old, she proved the doctors wrong once again. Not only did she survive, but from that day on, she thrived and progressed extremely well.

We pulled in the driveway, thrilled to bring our miracle girl home. As her father carried her into the house, I walked to the mailbox looking for any excuse to get some fresh air.

There it was. Right in front of me on the ground by my mailbox.

Another red quarter.

I cried and smiled. I looked up to Heaven and said, "I knew you were protecting *your girl* all along."

2011

Twelve years after Daddy passed, I received an opportunity to perform on stage.

The studio where I spent five days a week taking dance classes and later where I taught dance to dozens of little girls was having an alumni performance. They were celebrating their fiftieth year in business. Fifty years of teaching, training and inspiring young dancers. I was one of those lucky girls and absolutely loved dancing day after day, week after week, for many years.

I couldn't help but reminisce about dancing at that studio as a young girl. I remembered all those performances with my parents front and center, sitting in the audience. Daddy sat with a huge, proud smile on his face ready to clap and cheer for his baby girl.

Fondly thinking back to those days, I drove to rehearsal. I stopped at the store to get a drink and snacks for the hours backstage between performances. I was excited to dance once again after all these years.

I paid for my snacks and received my change. I looked down, and there it was…. another red quarter.

Convinced it was another message from Daddy, I could hear his voice in my mind.

I'm here with you, Pooh. I haven't missed a performance ever, and I won't miss this one either.

It reminded me of how proud he always was of me. My heart soared. I stood at the register with tears in my eyes and a big smile on my face. The cashier, surely wondering if he gave the correct change and what was so special about my quarter, asked if everything was okay.

"It's better now."

2014

Sammi, Daddy's oldest grandchild, was in fourth grade at Notre Dame Catholic School where all of our kids attended. Every day during lunch time, there was a snack cart for the kids to purchase a treat after lunch.

By this point, Sammi was well-versed in the amazing stories of the grandfather she never met. She even told one of her best friends, Marissa, about the red quarters.

Sammi, as kind as her mother, allowed a boy in front of her in line. As she moved up for her turn, she noticed the boy in front of her got a red quarter back with his change.

Excited and happy, she asked him if she could have just the red one and offered him a different quarter, in exchange for it. The boy refused. Sammi panicked and offered him a dollar for that red quarter, and he still said no.

On the verge of tears, Marissa explained the emotional story of why it was so important to her. Unfortunately, he still refused.

Still sad and emotional arriving home after school, she told Dawn the terrible events at the snack cart.

Dawn assured Sammi that it was her place in line and she did see it, so she was sure it was meant for her.

Two years later, having remembered the incident, Marissa found a red quarter and mailed it to Sammi.

2016

Going through a divorce is devastating. I gave all I had. I shared my life with him for close to twenty-three years. After building a life together having and raising two beautiful children, it was an extreme low for me. It should go without saying that it was a heart-breaking, difficult time. As I struggled to move on, I often reached out to my dearest friends who I knew would support me and listen with compassion.

One day in particular, I decided to stop and see an old friend. He had recently opened a new Pretzel Factory out of town, and I went for a drive to clear my head and ended up there.

As I arrived, he just so happened to have a few free moments to talk. I poured my heart out as I always had with TJ. He was always a great listener, supportive and compassionate, and still is to this day. We met my freshman year in highschool and have remained close over the years ever since. He's the type of friend that no matter how long we go without seeing each other or talking, we pick right up where we left off as if no time had passed.

I walked in, was greeted with a smile and was relieved to hear he just happened to have time to spare.

Although we'd been close friends for the past almost thirty years, he had never heard about the red quarters. Afterall, none of us had even thought about them since leaving Tuckerton and moving back to Vineland when I was twelve years old.

I talked about the divorce and how much I'd been struggling emotionally to forgive and move on. I talked about Daddy. It was the first time I allowed the thought of *it's a good thing he's not here* to cross my mind. Daddy would have been so devastated that his little girl had to endure a divorce. TJ knew him very well since we spent so much time together during high school. I explained how badly, especially at a time like this in my life, I needed him right now. I shared stories about going to the arcade in Tuckerton. I told him about the red quarters Mommy and Daddy had painted for Dawn and I to play with there.

And with that, TJ opened his register and said, "Like this?"

He held a red quarter. The surprise left me frozen and speechless which, he agreed, was a rare thing. Tears filled my eyes, and a smile stretched widely across my face as I reached out to feel the red quarter in my fingers. What made it even more impactful, even for TJ, was that he had no idea about the red quarters and their connection with Daddy since his death.

At that moment, I was again reminded that Daddy is with me. He knows what's happening in my life and chooses a trusted friend to deliver his support and love from beyond.

2017

Daddy often used other people in our lives to let us know he was with us. Just like when he was still with us, he always did anything in his power to show his love for us.

Many people in our lives have never heard of or seen a red quarter. Keeping Daddy alive in our hearts, certain situations would remind us of him, and we'd proudly tell our friends about our amazing father and the red quarters.

Dawn was sharing stories of her father one day in the school faculty lounge.

Dawn has been a terrific art teacher for more than twenty years, and Daddy always bragged to everyone about her artistic ability.

She had created close friendships with faculty and staff during her many years at Rieck Avenue Elementary School, so it was natural for her to become fast friends with Corey, her student-teacher.

Touched by the stories of the red quarters, Corey created a monoprint of one. On the quarter, he included the opening date of Obsession.

Six months later, Corey sent Dawn an image attached to his text. He was holding a red quarter in his hand. The text read, *This is for you.*

He had gone to the Philadelphia Museum of Art with his girlfriend and was just telling her about what a positive influence Dawn has made on his life. Just then, he was fumbling for change in the console of his car when there it was…

A red quarter.

He had never before seen or heard of one until hearing Dawn's stories. Excited to see her at school Monday morning, he handed it to her with a smile and said, "I am pretty sure *this* was meant for *you*."

Oftentimes, we've experienced people that have never heard of or seen a red quarter receive one after hearing about our wonderful memories of Daddy. It confirms for us the belief that our friends intercept Daddy's message in order to give it to us. What's especially heartwarming about such a transaction is the belief it creates with them regarding their own passed loved ones.

Lisa, a secretary at Dawn's school, had such an experience.

Running late for work one morning, Lisa scrambled to get the kids out the door on time. Making lunches for her children was the usual routine, but this morning there was no time. Having no other option, she quickly dug her hand into the family coin jar to give them money to buy lunch. Lisa rushed her children out of the house and turned around to return the extra coins to the Mason jar. To her surprise, she spotted a red quarter.

She had never seen a red quarter prior to that morning, hearing Dawn's stories just the day before at school.

That morning, Dawn was thrilled to receive another red quarter through a dear friend.

2018

Whenever I'm in the midst of difficult times, I often think of Daddy, remembering how his love, support and guidance would provide so much comfort.

My grandmother's, our sweet Nonni's, health was failing fast. It was torture watching her slowly decline. I thought of Daddy, remembering his suffering and how he quickly went downhill toward the end. I'm reminded of him whenever I am dealt the torture of witnessing a loved one's illness. Again, like countless other times in my life, I needed my Daddy to wrap his arms around me and to help me through this terrible situation.

After a typical Friday after teaching for the day, I headed to visit Nonni. I felt anxious and apprehensive to see her with each passing day but aware that I needed to spend as much time with her as possible. Just before leaving school, I checked my mailbox in the faculty lounge. Usually, I check my mail in the mornings. A large interoffice mail package was sticking out of the box. I noticed the sender's name. My dear friend, Lori, sent a note. She works at another school within the district which makes it easy to send items through interoffice mail.

The note read:

> *My Dear Gina,*
>
> *I had such a tickle in my throat, so I went to our faculty room to buy a bottle of water from our vending machine which I NEVER do as I always bring my own, and this red quarter from 1980 popped out with my change. I immediately smiled and took*

it as a sign from 'Daddy' to send this to you today. I hope it puts a big smile on your face as it did mine. I know you're having a tough time with Nonni, but apparently, your dad wants you to know he's here and all will be alright.

Love you-

Lori XO

That was perfect timing.

I smiled as a tear rolled down my cheek. The warmth of Daddy's presence overwhelmed me once more. The reassurance that once again he was with me. Peace brought a smile to my face. He was with me as I visited Nonni and with her as she suffered. I believe he met Nonni in Heaven when her time came.

2018

It was Faith's first dance recital.

I was so proud of her first year of dance classes. The nostalgia of her attending my childhood studio made it even more thrilling for me.

The special needs dance class was a new addition to the studio's roster. All the children tried their best at weekly classes and, more importantly, felt accepted and loved. An amazing, happy experience was had by all.

Faith and I rushed down the hall with bags of hair and makeup, costumes over my shoulder.

I reminisced about the numerous years of such experiences throughout my own life. Remembering Mommy and Daddy proudly seated front and center in the audience as usual.

Just then, I noticed it there on the floor. I stopped so abruptly that I dropped the bags and costumes on the floor.

It was another red quarter for Faith and me.

Daddy was letting us know once again that he had never and would never miss a dance recital for one of *his girls*.

Faith stole the show, running out of her assigned spot to the very front edge of the stage. Her arms waved in the air, and she laughed out loud with a huge smile on her face. I felt exhilarated and sure that Daddy was with us, clapping and smiling with pride.

2019

There were many situations in life where I would receive a red quarter and be unsure of his message. They are always during a wonderful phase of my life or an extremely difficult one. It's sometimes difficult to discern his intention.

Was he just saying, "I'm here with you. I see what you're going through."?

Maybe he means to say, "Yes. That's a great idea." Or is the red quarter a warning not to go ahead with a specific decision?

I was excited to go away for the weekend. As we packed the last few items in the luggage, I heard John open the safe in the next room. I dismissed it, thinking he grabbed extra cash for the trip.

As we headed down the road, we made our usual Wawa stop for coffee. He paid at the register and shoved the change he received from the cashier into his pocket.

I thought nothing of it.

As we returned to the truck, he pulled the bulky change from his jeans and tossed it into the console. I looked and squealed with delight. "Baby, you got a red quarter!"

It crossed my mind that it meant something wonderful was going to happen on our weekend getaway. I knew he got 'something' from his safe earlier. I then wondered if maybe it was a ring.

I felt as though Daddy was sending him a message and felt thrilled that he gave it to John.

We were engaged on the beach in Maryland two days later.

2021

Moving back to Vineland after a year of living in Pitman felt 'right'. I was home. My second husband, John, and I bought our first home together. It was a beautiful, white rancher on a full acre of land. Our home, filled with several cousins, dear friends and other family members, was a bustle of activity as we all cleaned and moved in the furniture.

Before I knew it, that house was our charming new home. I loved our little farmhouse.

I sat surrounded by fields of peppers and grape orchards. In our own yard, we built a huge garden complete with everything from tomatoes to zucchini to pumpkins and more. I had eight beautiful chickens whom I affectionately named and chatted with daily.

We installed a large, above-ground pool, and the sun glistened on the water. As the ladies free-ranged and pecked around in the yard, I sat in front of forty-seven acres of gorgeous farmland. The sun rose above the fields just behind my backyard and casted burnt orange light on the clear blue pool water. I sipped my coffee and enjoyed God's wonder.

Unfortunately, that joy didn't last for very long. Two years later, John left.

Life is filled with challenges. The one thing you can expect is for the unexpected to happen. And always when you least expect it.

I allowed myself to believe this would never happen. I was heartbroken and devastated. I felt betrayed. It was hard to make sense of what took place. Suddenly, I went from happy and grateful to heartbroken and terrified. Struggling financially, I sold my beloved rancher on a farm.

I was about to lose my home, financially destitute, shattered emotionally and teaching full time.

I have a grown son that I want to inspire and teach about rising strong when life beats you down. I have the challenge, although filled with many joys, of raising a child with Down syndrome. I'm overwhelmed. I feel lost.

My thoughts raced, and my heartbeat quickened.

My husband left after seven years together. I sat on my back deck with my coffee and watched the golden sun rise. I talk to Daddy often on mornings like this and pray for guidance. I then asked,

"Daddy, where are you? What are you doing up there? Don't you see what I'm going through? Please help me. How has my life turned out this way? I need you."

I closed my eyes and then asked God to guide my thoughts, words and actions. I thought about what Daddy would say if he were here with me now.

Daddy never lectured. He never told me exactly what to do. He would look at me with compassion and understanding as he listened to the issue at hand. Reassured me with confidence and reminded me how much he believed in me.

To have someone believe in you more than you believe in yourself is empowering. It creates the will to dig deep and find the courage to face whatever comes your way. Whenever I was feeling down, he could always lift my spirits and guide me to stand on my own two feet with my head held high. I felt capable of tackling the next challenge in life.

I felt desperate to hear his voice, to have him look into my eyes with that smile and that unwavering confidence in my abilities. I sat quietly and continued to pray.

Then, it came to me. I realized that I knew just what Daddy would say to me.

You are strong and worthy of wonderful things. I know it's hard, but you will be okay, Pooh. God sees your struggle and is sending you down a new path. Trust and believe in Him.

The next day, I drove to the nearby convenience store for a few odds and ends. I stood at the register in relief. I had hoped for this. I needed it. And there it was. Another red quarter in the palm of my hand along with the rest of my change. The owner of the store asked why the red one was so special. He noticed the tears in my eyes as I stared at it.

I told him the short version of Daddy's quarters from Heaven. He said that in all his years of owning that store, he had never seen a red quarter. I said it was because I just moved here and Daddy followed me. He smiled.

I desperately wanted confirmation that Daddy heard my conversation with him and God the day before, and there it was.

Once more before leaving my farmhouse, I went to that same convenience store. I was teaching Faith about money, so I sent her to the register to pay. The owner greeted us excitedly, "You got another one!"

As Faith handed him the bills, he placed the change, including another red quarter, in her little hand. He looked at her and said, "It's from your poppop."

My heart leapt for Faith getting her first red quarter from her Poppop Sal.

It really helped me to find some peace during what was an extremely difficult time for me. I slowly remembered how to fight, how to love myself and do as my Daddy taught me… move on with my head held high.

At fifty-two years old, I finally know my worth. I am a good Christian, a devoted mother, a loving daughter and sister. I'm a great teacher and have always made my students' needs a priority. I'm loyal and kind. I wear my heart on my sleeve. I am smart and capable. There was a fork in my road, and God led me down the path that is meant for me.

2022

Sea Isle City holds special memories for our family.

Year after year, we'd stay there for a week every summer with Mommy, Daddy, Nonni and Poppop. As young children, we'd stay another week with our close friends as well.

Memories of walking the promenade with friends, the bright lights and the loud music of the amusement rides are unforgettable.

As the days went on, Daddy's and my olive skin got darker with ease. Mommy and Dawn, on the other hand, always ended up lobster red by the end of each day.

Remembering Obsession so many years ago, Daddy loved bringing *his girls* to play in the arcade at the Spinnaker building. It was just as fun for us as young adults remembering our sweet childhood memories in our own arcade.

So naturally, as moms, Dawn and I continue to go with our own children.

Dawn had her own condo in the Spinnaker for a couple years, so they frequented that arcade almost daily. Sammi and Luke went through dozens of quarters as Dawn smiled, wrapped up in her memories. Dawn stood talking with the owner, Ryan, reminiscing about Obsession and the red quarters.

Ryan loved the sentimental stories and said, "After all my years running this arcade, I have never seen one."

On their last day of vacation, Dawn returned to the arcade under their Spinnaker condo with Sammi and Luke. They passed by the game that pushes quarters to the very edge until they fall through the opening of the machine that spat out dozens of winning tickets. It's an all-time favorite. Stopping in their tracks, Sammi grabbed her mother's arm.

"Mom. Look!" A red quarter tucked under several others was barely hanging on to the edge.

Ryan approached after hearing Sammi exclaim and noticed Dawn and her kids. He quickly came over with a smile on his face, keys in hand. He carefully opened the glass cover so as not to lose the coveted coin down the metal shoot. Ryan carefully plucked it from within and handed Daddy's greeting to his youngest grandson.

The next summer, Dawn and the kids returned to the arcade as usual. Ryan approached her with a bucket in hand.

"After hearing your stories, all of a sudden, red quarters came through here again and again! I kept them separate and saved them for you and his grandkids."

Flashback 1966-recent

My cousin, Kimmy, was about four or five years old, thrilled to be cruising 'the Ave' in my mom's new convertible. Mommy spotted Daddy and a friend on the sidewalk.

She whispered to Kimmy, "Be good, okay? I really like this guy."

They pulled into a parking spot, and Sammy noticed and approached the car with a smile. He leaned in the window to say hello.

Looking at the adorable passenger, he asked, "And what's your name?"

Little Kimmy, not wanting to make a mistake or say anything wrong, quickly said, "Nobody."

Daddy laughed and said, "Well hello, Nobody."

'Nobody' was the flower girl at their wedding about a year later.

The nickname stuck. Daddy and Kimmy always had a special connection. They called each other 'Nobody' for the rest of his life.

Many years after Daddy had passed, Kimmy was with her husband, Mark, at their favorite pizza place with some friends. They were discussing a possible business partnership in none other than an *arcade*.

Kimmy and Mark felt uneasy about the endeavor but heard them out as they explained the offer. In her gut, she thought it might be a mistake.

Kimmy went to the register to pay for their pizza. She received her change and was shocked when she looked down and saw a red quarter in her hand.

She took it as a sign not to go ahead with the business project as she always took the advice of her 'nobody'.

2024

Dawn recently was forced to move when the landlord decided to sell the home she was renting.

She is a hard-working, single mom that puts everyone else's needs above her own. Dawn was careful to save as much of her money as she could, while working full-time and driving back and forth to Pennsylvania quite often. Her youngest child, Luke, is now seventeen years old and playing basketball for his high school team and a travel team. Driving him to games and out-of-state tournaments and picking him up to bring him home from his dorm kept her extremely busy.

She luckily found a great condo for her, Sammi and Luke.

Like me, Dawn always thinks of Daddy and often talks to him during a difficult time in her life. Packing up and moving for the second time within the past year proved to add to her stress and worry.

The condo was filled with our family and friends dedicated to assisting with moving in countless boxes and bins. We were all there to help as she always had for each of us when needed.

Dawn was overwhelmed and a bit emotional as to be expected. She set a box of kitchen items on the dining room table and began removing the pots, pans and utensils. She had packed that box herself just days ago from the old house.

She stopped and stared a moment. At the very bottom, looking up at her was another red quarter.

Dawn keeps all her red quarters tucked safely away in a special jar.

For a second, she thought, *How did that get here?*

She reached down to grab it, squeezed it tight and held it against her heart.

"Thank you for being here, Daddy."

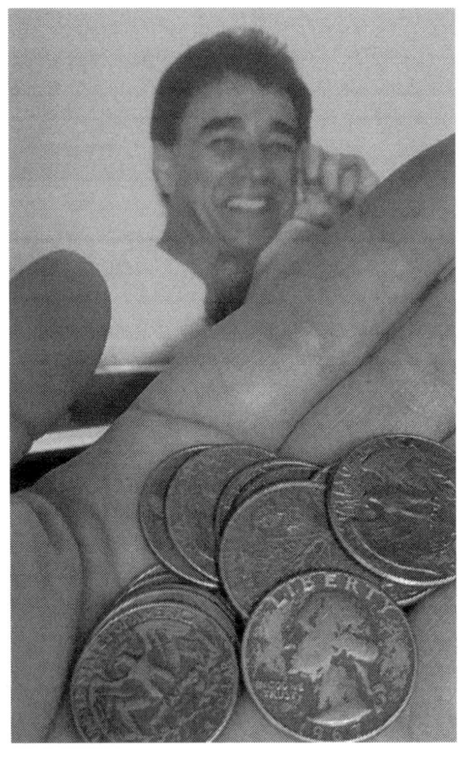

Actual Red Quarters Daddy's pic

CHAPTER 12

Love Transcends Time and Space

After twenty-five years, I still miss Daddy immensely. I see him in my mind so clearly. I close my eyes and ask him to guide me throughout my life. Countless times, I've ached for him to be here on Earth. Times of pure joy, I can still feel his presence. When a season of pain and struggle enter my life, I wish he could tell me what to do.

It is during those difficult times that I often hear his voice from deep within my heart. It's as if he knows and is listening to me beg for help during prayer. I then clearly see the expression on his face, the familiar eye roll and the crooked smirk as if to say, *Really, Pooh bear? Pull yourself together. You got this babe. I believe in you.*

I find myself thinking that my father deserved more.

A man of integrity.

A loyal, generous husband.

An honest, hardworking banker.

A devoted family man.

A fun-loving, trustworthy friend.

A father who would do anything and absolutely adored *his girls*.

Without a doubt, he deserved more. He deserved more than struggling to make ends meet. He deserved more than the stress of wondering if his job was going to be there the next day with mergers always looming. He deserved more than a steady dose of stress worrying about supporting his family.

Now that I'm an adult with similar struggles, I can imagine him breaking down to my mother to hear her supportive and loving encouragement. Her steadfast love carried him through the difficult times. Her smile made him feel as though it was all worth it. I, personally, never heard him complain. As hard as it may be to believe, he never took his stress out on *his girls*. He forged on, day after day, content with the love of his family and friends and enjoyed the somewhat serious card games with family on weekends. He was uplifted by fun times and laughter with friends. And without a doubt, he lived for the opportunities to watch *his girls* perform, succeed and enjoy the life that he provided for us.

He deserved more than a two-year, tortuous battle with cancer which, ultimately, was the last challenge he had to face.

It breaks my heart that a man like him had such a terrible end to the wonderful, selfless life he led.

I do know, however, that even at the end, he felt as if it was all worth it.

I know this because I can still see his face light up when he was with his family, clearly forgetting all troubles and, obviously, grateful for his beautiful wife, his life, his family and his friends.

I have no doubt that if given the chance to come back to Earth knowing he'd suffer in the end again, he would do it all over to have even one more day with *his girls*.

He was a loving, patient father who taught me valuable lessons I still apply to my life all these years later. And even after his death, he still teaches me. To be grateful for what matters most in life. To accept struggles and stress as a part of life. To be okay with it because it affords you the most precious gifts of all. Not money or expensive things. Not a fancy car or mansion on the shore. But that it is all okay when you have special people to love and how it's all worth it because you are blessed to have them love you back.

He left this Earth at the young age of fifty-six. I can't tell you how many times over the past twenty-five years I've uttered the words, *It's so unfair. He's missed out on so much. I wish he was still here.*

He never got to meet any of his grandchildren. He was so excited to become a grandfather one day. At the time of his passing, Dawn and I had both just gotten married, and he was already talking about his grandkids and everything he would do with them.

Having been so blessed to have him as an amazing father, there is no doubt that he would have made a wonderful, fun, loving and present grandfather. He surely would have been *grand*.

I've cried countless times over the years. It never matters how long he's been gone. It still hurts. I ache for him. There is, without a doubt, a gaping hole in my life that I wish he could still fill.

He missed his first grandchild, Samantha, Sammi, named after him, by only two months. He was so excited about having grandchildren and another little one to refer to as *his girl*.

He missed out on her volleyball games and watching her athletic talent develop. He missed her dance recitals, great report cards, high school performances and her graduation. He wasn't there to attempt to scare off her boyfriend as he would then immediately make him part of our family. And he wasn't there to see her get her psychology degree and move on to her masters.

He missed his first grandson's birth. My son who carries his name as Matthew Salvatore.

He wasn't there when he walked and talked before a year old, caught his first ball, took karate or played soccer. He missed out on his throw from third to first at the age of seven. He wasn't there to watch all the baseball games or when he was the closing pitcher that won the tournament. He missed out on helping him learn how to drive, his high school graduation, moving to West Virginia and getting his first job. He never got to revel in what an amazing protector he is for his little sister, Faith, and bask in his unwavering love for his special sibling.

He missed out on watching my nephew, Luke, grow up with such a big heart, kind like him. He wasn't there to watch as he grew taller than his parents. He didn't cheer him on courtside as he became an awesome basketball player. He missed countless basketball games and tournaments. He's not here to brag about his Division I scholarship offers either.

He missed the six excruciating weeks of Faith in the NICU having been born six weeks early, on a feeding tube and waiting for surgery. He wasn't there when I paced the hallway outside of the waiting room, praying the rosary as she underwent open-heart surgery at only five months old. He missed the chance to cheer her on as she pulled out her own feeding tube on Easter morning and ate on her own like a champ, proving all the doctors wrong. He missed Faith walking for the first time, running, playing, learning her numbers, letters and colors, proving that a child with Down syndrome can do amazing things. I cried again when she rode a horse for the first time and again as she danced on stage, remembering all the years my Daddy was front and center cheering on his own little ballerina.

He wasn't there for me when I was betrayed and divorced after more than twenty years. He didn't put his arms around me as I cried to assure me that I would be okay. He wasn't there as I put my heart on the line again and had it shattered once more.

He wasn't there for Dawn as she experienced the same heartbreak. He's not here to help her navigate herself through a terrible divorce or to make her believe she can start a new life for herself.

He missed out on consoling Mommy when she lost her parents. He wasn't there as she cried over missing him all these years.

Or was he?

For years, I felt sad for myself, for each of us and for him over all of the above. I thought he missed out, but then I realized he was, in fact, here. He was there for all of us all along. His love is so powerful that he managed to send messages to prove his spirit was with us.

He has wrapped his arms around us during every heartbreak.

He has cheered along with every victory his grandchildren achieved.

He has roared his typical, fun-loving, boisterous laugh at every birthday, graduation and holiday party.

God has allowed him to be present and prove that he didn't miss one single precious moment.

Every cardinal at just the right moment said, *I am here with you.* Every 'Sal' sign traveling on vacations reminded me he was with us. Every time the Dallas mug is grabbed from the back of the cabinet by an unknowing guest, and on his birthday no less. He's saying, *I'm here, Pooh.*

But without question, the most convincing evidence has been our precious *red quarters.*

The red quarters he and my mother painted for us to use in our own arcade when we were just children, that no one else knew about.

The red quarters we never saw again, or thought about for decades, after closing the business and moving more than an hour away.

The red quarters special to just Daddy and *his girls* that only resurfaced after his passing.

The red quarters have been 'given to us', sent down from Heaven on days of sadness and days of pure joy.

Received on days that one may think he missed out on and always given when we wanted and needed him the most. Sad times of loss, difficult times during extreme stress and celebratory life events are all those times when you want the people you love the most to be with you. My father was always with us when it mattered most in life. I submit that the true stories in this book that took place over many years for several different people in various circumstances after my father's death are proof that he is still with us.

Many of you resonate with my grief. You have battled with the sorrow of having lost a parent. Some of you can absolutely relate because you lost a child, sibling, a dear friend or someone with whom you had a deep connection.

And for that, I am truly sorry.

The immense loss creates a terrible void that we long to fill. Our person had a piece of our heart. Remember, though, that space we held just for them remains still. They had a special home in our hearts that brought us immense joy, fulfillment, happiness and love. Although they have left this Earth, we don't truly lose them. We keep them in our hearts. We can choose to hold that space just for them. That is where their memories and our love for them reside. Hold on to that. Visit that place in your heart as often as needed.

I thought of you often in writing this book. I know you understand and maybe even shed another tear as you read about my personal experiences.

Although it's painful, some days more than others, knowing someone 'gets it' provides a bit of comfort. Through grief, we are somehow united. Only we can truly understand the depths of despair, the unbearable emptiness and the heartbreak of knowing they are no longer with us on this Earth. We share similar stories of love, loss, grief and coping.

You will miss them every single day of your life. Holidays, birthdays and special occasions cause setbacks. Your father, mother, sibling, lover or friend was part of your heart. We miss their physical presence, but the connection remains.

Be open to their spiritual presence. They are with us in times of struggle still supporting us, sending their love and support from beyond. The void you feel is evidence of their powerful impact.

I remember that feeling, as if a bolt of lightning struck my heart. As I moved past denial and let myself acknowledge the pain of losing him, the healing began.

Time does help to ease the pain. The scar remains as a gift. It's the mark they left on our lives, their stamp to say, *I was here, I loved you, and I will always be with you.*

How amazing is our God to bless us with such an amazing person? How understanding and loving is our God to allow Daddy to bless us with peace and love from heaven?

The best gifts for me are Heaven-sent… the gifts of *the red quarters.*

He wasn't perfect. He liked to play the lottery. So much so that he would get up in the middle of dinner to 'get his tickets'. He'd take money from his own family at a weekly game of cards while eating homemade pasta and dunking his biscotti into his coffee. He smoked too much and cussed occasionally although never in front of *his girls.*

But…

He'd do anything for his family and friends. He was loyal to the core. His laugh was a contagious roar that bellowed from rooms away. His smile could light up any room. He could calm your fears with the touch of his hand, and he loved *his girls* with his entire heart.

He may not have been perfect, but to me…

He was *everything*.

We are always searching for confirmation that our loved one is okay. We always hope that they are somehow still with us, walking among us, making sure we are safe. Whether it's a cardinal that seems to visit at just the right moment or an unexpected feather as if a precious gift from an angel just when we need it the most. Maybe it's a sign on the side of the road that happens to have the name of our loved one right after we are missing them and thinking about our good times together. It may be their favorite song on the radio or their favorite team winning the Super Bowl that gives you the overwhelming feeling of their presence.

For me, it has been the gifts of the red quarters. Always when I need it the most. Always at times he would have been there cheering me on or holding my hand through difficulty.

My hope is that in reading my story, where you once had doubt in your mind, you now have peace in your heart with the knowledge that not only are they in a better place, but their spirit is with us and may even visit from time to time.

Acknowledgements

There are countless contributors that have helped me along my journey of completing this book.

First and foremost, I'd like to give thanks and praise to God for enabling Daddy to drop those precious Red Quarters on our path when we missed and needed him the most in our lives. Thank You for putting this dream of writing in my heart. Thank You for showing me the way when I struggled to get my ideas onto the paper. Without Your answered prayers and blessings, I never would have been able to complete this book.

To my son, Matthew Salvatore. You are more than just a supportive, loving son and an amazing big brother. You are also a terrific editor. You have become a reliable confidant, a person with whom I can bounce off ideas and have meaningful conversations about life, writing and how to make improvements without losing my voice as an author. I am truly grateful for your extensive knowledge, hard work and friendship. You remind me so much of my Daddy with your kind heart, patience and similar handsome features. I am so thankful we have shared in the writing of your grandfather's life and that you had this opportunity to learn even more about him throughout our writing journey.

To my daughter, Faith, who brought me several cups of coffee during every writing session and who displayed great patience having to wait for Mommy to play with her because I was busy writing.

Both of you, my sweet children, are my inspiration to always learn more, love big and do better.

To my beautiful Mommy, words are not enough to express my appreciation of you. Thank you for the wonderful marriage you nurtured with Daddy and for exemplifying the true meaning of 'soulmates'. Your countless afternoons of babysitting as I wrote this book are greatly appreciated. I cherish your constant love and support.

To my big sis, Dawny, I don't know where to begin. You have always been by my side through the ups and downs of my entire life. Most of my memories of life with Daddy included you. Thank you for the many hours of listening to rewrites and deep conversations sharing your memories of Daddy. You have laughed and cried with me, taken me by the hand and led me down memory lane in order to complete this book with accurate anecdotes and precious memories. I am forever grateful. Your confidence in me enabled me to believe in myself. I'd be lost without you.

To the rest of 'my kids', Sammi, Luke and Michael, I cannot thank you enough for being the best 'cheering section' a girl could ever have. Your support, praise, unconditional love and steady belief in me truly encouraged me to forge ahead.

To 'my girls', my best friends, who are more like family, thank you is surely not enough. You have been there through the good, the not-so-good and the terrible times supporting me and both of my children in any way you could. Thank you for your praise and support of my writing. I'm so grateful for your countless displays of love and encouragement.

Dear Daddy,

Thank you. Even though you haven't been with us on this Earth for twenty-five years, I know you are with me in spirit. I can hear your words of encouragement. Thank you for always being supportive of all my endeavors. I know you would be proud of the fact that your Poohbear is sharing our story. I cannot thank you enough for your unconditional love and unwavering support throughout my life which was the inspiration for this book. I am the person I am today because of you.

During the past twenty-five years, I have often struggled and desperately missed you. I know you are still with your girls. *And always will be. I often feel your presence, and in my mind, I can still see 'the look'-your eyes wide and your crooked smirk trying to hold back laughter. Because after all… your love transcends time and space.*

Love,

Poohbear

About the Author

Gina Panzino is not just an author; she's also a single mom of two incredible kids, a full-time teacher, and a group fitness instructor. Her book, Have a Little Faith, showcases her daughter's incredible accomplishments despite having Down syndrome. Gina is also the author of the adult nonfiction book, Raising Faith: The Ups and Downs of Raising a Child with Down Syndrome. In addition, Gina is a certified health and life coach who writes two blogs with the goal of inspiring and motivating people to achieve inner balance and cultivate self-love. Gina focuses on supporting, motivating, and uplifting others through her content. You can learn more about Gina Panzino at www.ginapanzino.com.

Review Ask

Did you love this book?

Please consider leaving a review!

Every review matters. You can go to Amazon, or wherever you purchased this book to inform future readers of the benefit.

Made in the USA
Columbia, SC
06 October 2024

7981b780-2c34-4ef9-9c19-59710e609e14R01